Scilly Birding

Joining the Madding Crowd

Scilly Birding

Joining the Madding Crowd

Simon Davey

Brambleby Books

Scilly Birding – Joining the Madding Crowd
Copyright © Simon Davey 2013

*Simon Davey has asserted his right
under the Copyright, Designs and Patents Act 1988
to be identified as the Author of this Work.*

All Rights Reserved

*No part of this book may be reproduced in any form
by photocopying or by any electronic or mechanical means,
including information, storage or retrieval systems,
without permission in writing from both the copyright
owner and the publisher of this book.*

A CIP catalogue record for this book is available from the British Library

ISBN 978-1-908241-17-7
eISBN 978-1-908241-26-9

First published in 2013 by BRAMBLEBY BOOKS
Reprint in 2016

www.bramblebybooks.co.uk

Cover design and layout by Tanya Warren – Creatix
Cover photo by Simon Davey
©Illustrations and map by Amanda Davey

Printed and bound in Great Britain by
Clays Ltd, St Ives plc

Dedication

To my wife Amanda, whose patience with my many absences and hours in front of a telescope has been amazing. She is responsible for the drawings in the book and for giving me constant support.

Contents

	Preface	11
	About the Author	15
Chapter 1	Preparations	17
Chapter 2	The journey down	23
Chapter 3	First impressions of Scilly… and some good birds	33
Chapter 4	Birds, birds…and more birds	43
Chapter 5	A quiet day on Scilly…almost	61
Chapter 6	The Yellowthroat…and how we suffered for it	73
Chapter 7	A much better day…after a bad start	83
Chapter 8	The Swainson's Thrush…and the Great Grip Off!!	95
Chapter 9	Two quiet days…It happens, even on Scilly	107
Chapter 10	More birds arrive in the Scilly Islands…at last	113
Chapter 11	Return to St. Agnes…and yet more fine weather	125
Chapter 12	Back to Tresco…this time, a much more successful visit	133
Chapter 13	Plans that go like clock work…perhaps this is the Scilly answer?	143
Chapter 14	The day of the long wait…followed by a dip	161
Chapter 15	My last day in the Scilly Isles…during 1984 at least	173
Chapter 16	The return journey	181
	Postscript	187
	Acknowledgements	188
	References Cited in Text – Further Reading	189

Preface

"Your husband is being magnificent!" Startled, I watched the lady rushing happily towards me coming up the steps. Waiting for news after a coach breakdown in Oman, that reaction was a bit unexpected. They had been stuck in the searing heat for four and a half hours and were expected to be both de-hydrated and exhausted from the heat. Apparently, while a naval commander took control of the bathroom situation, Simon and a friend of his had been showing anyone who was interested the birds that they were sitting next to for all of this time. When he came back, he was grinning from ear to ear. He had seen several new birds, having hardly noticed the conditions at all. Those not interested in the birds had enjoyed the spectacle of his dedication to watching birds in the dusty air.

Simon and I met in late 1983. At this stage he was a classic example of the museum broad-range naturalist, interested and knowledgeable in all groups, with botany probably the key interest. He was a member of the local ornithological club, which he enjoyed but not ostentatiously. I breathed a sigh of relief having spent a childhood enduring Sunday afternoon duck watching without being particularly inspired by any of them.

Then, in mid-1984 two key things happened. A Two-barred Crossbill turned up in the New Forest and someone lent him a copy of Bill Oddie's *Little Black Bird Book*. We ambled with curiosity up to where the new bird had been seen to find a big gang of binocular-clad, wax-jacket festooned people with a bit of a mad glint on their faces. Suddenly up went a whoop and the adrenaline punctured the air. Looking back sheepishly, he was hooked! The rush of excitement and enthusiasm was infectious. The birds were flitting high in the pine trees, making them very elusive. That day he saw no Two-barred Crossbill, but two days later not only had he seen it, but he had started to plan his first trip to the Isles of Scilly! This book is the story of that trip and the voyage of discovery into this mad, frenetic world of twitching.

In the years since that time, we as a couple have visited some of the strangest back streets of strange and unexpected towns and villages following twitch after twitch. Many and various rubbish dumps have been involved. I have managed huge volumes of reading which has helped keep on top of professional journals. Simon has managed a bird list that quickly reached the then key 400, although he isn't as active on the twitching scene as he once was.

My best memory of a twitch I attended was an accident of fate in Norfolk. We were taking Simon's mother for a gentle bird-watching weekend around the Holkham area. On the Friday night, he looked at her apologetically and said, "I'll just see what's about." He dashed off to find the nearest phone box. Mobile phones were still largely a thing of the future. Moments later, he came rushing back. "There's a Mega!! There's a Mega!!…Sorry Mum, do you mind?? There's only a Mega!!" A Red-breasted Nuthatch had been seen at dusk in Holkham Pines. There really wasn't an answer to the question, and we had little choice but to go and join the growing throng early the following morning. I have never experienced anything like it before…nor since. Quite literally thousands of twitchers were there on that day. It was more like a rock concert in the woods than the quiet bird watching weekend I had had in mind! My mother-in-law and I sat next to each other on a log and had a lovely few hours chatting about all manner of things, while meanwhile seas of booted and waxed, tripod-wielding maniacs thudded past us in waves, first going one way, then back again in the other direction. No whoops or cries, just thud, thud, thud. In retrospect, it was almost exactly the same idea as the scene in one of the *Inspector Clouseau* films where the old drunk is trying to cross the road, as Clouseau and the baddies chase each other, with a sports car turning up from time to time. I know I am biased, but I do think of him waving as he zoomed past us just like that sports car.

Amanda Davey March 2013

About the Author

Simon Davey was born in Kent and educated at King's School, Ely (where he was a cathedral chorister) and then at Selwyn College, Cambridge. Being the son of a schoolmaster living in the grounds of a former stately home in Norfolk, natural history was his passion from his earliest days. A shout of "Clouded Yellow" would cause instant pandemonium and net searching throughout the house. His father was an avid collector of butterflies and moths, and birds were only a minor interest before his introduction to a Two-barred Crossbill in the New Forest, his first ever 'twitch'. After teaching biology and chemistry for a short while, he entered the museums profession as a biologist. For many years he was keeper of Biology at the Hampshire County Museum Service, as well as curator of the Red House Museum in Christchurch. In 1988, he became an independent consultant ecologist specialising in botany, particularly lichens. This independence also allowed him to lead natural history holidays to various parts of the world, including Central Asia, Central and South America, as well as the Galapagos Islands, the Arctic, the Mediterranean and Spain. It has also given him time for birding and for travelling the length and breadth of Britain looking for rare avian visitors. He has also lectured many times on cruise ships, destinations including Chile, Peru, Ecuador and the Caribbean, as well as Madeira, the Canary Islands, the Middle East and the Red Sea, the Baltic, the Mediterranean, Iceland, Norway, northern Spitzbergen, Greenland and North Africa. Although birding has been a favourite pastime for many years, professionally he specialises in lichens, and his interests and knowledge of the natural world are diverse and range from plants and the history of botany to insects, birds and especially whales, and include arctic landscapes and volcanoes.

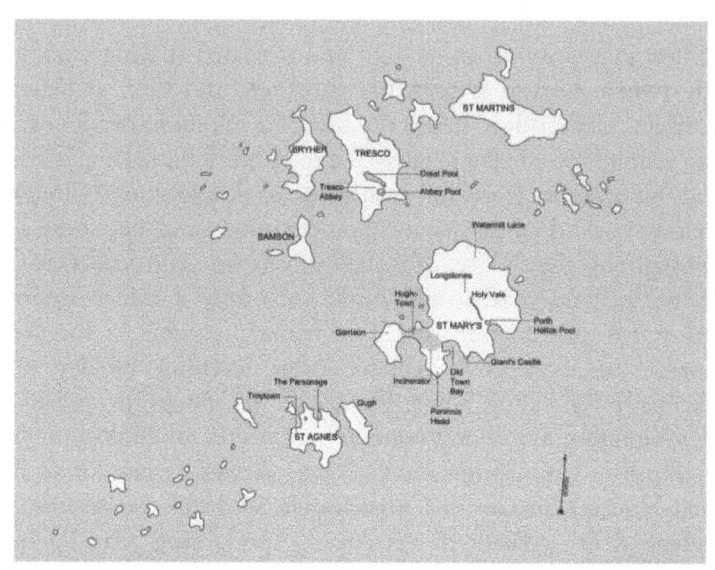

Map of the Isles of Scilly

1. Preparations

Question: What twitches and ticks, and rushes round the Isles of Scilly in October?
Answer: A Scilly Birder!

A 'twitcher' is someone who will travel vast distances at the drop of a hat. In former days (i.e. the mid-1980s, which this narrative concerns), before the advent of mobile communication devices, this strange behaviour was more usually triggered by a landline phone call to go and see rare birds...that is *RARE* birds. What sends a twitcher into ecstasies is adding new ticks to his or her lists of birds. Some ticks are more important than others. If they are a first personal sighting they are called 'lifers'. They can be a first for Britain, Europe, the world or even the garden. They may be the first for that year, or month. In fact, birders make lists for almost anything. In America, fanatical birders are called listers. I have heard of several birders who have a crap list; they list birds they have seen relieving themselves. Others even teletick, having a list of species they have seen on the television.

In some circles twitcher is a term of abuse, but few people interested in birds, known nowadays as birders rather than birdwatchers, are just concerned with adding ticks to their lists; most are passionately interested in the study and habits of the birds they go off to see. Some wouldn't be seen dead with the title of 'twitcher' associated with their name. However, most birders will admit to twitching, even if only ever so occasionally.

In those days, I used to belong to a group of naturalists called the Christchurch Harbour Ornithological Group, known affectionately as CHOG: members are Choggers. Chog is an active group and has many young members. They work the salt marsh and harbour near Christchurch and Hengistbury Head. This is an excellent area for birds, especially during the spring and autumn migration. The group holds indoor meetings during the winter, after which we all dash off for a less formal and distinctly more liquid session in the Plumber's Arms, our local.

Over a second, or was it a third pint, the 1983 Scilly Choggers told the rest of us about the amazing birds they had seen on Scilly. Two firsts for the Western Palaearctic! In a fortnight? That's absurd. Perhaps I had had too much to drink, and there was still half an hour before closing time. A Green Warbler and a Cliff Swallow! That's not only absurd, it's positively greedy! They mentioned, not quite in passing, the Rose-breasted Grosbeak they had found themselves, the Parula Warbler, the Bobolink on the grass in the centre of town which fed with sparrows, and the Upland Sandpiper which took food from the hand. By this time I was completely lost. I hadn't even heard of most of these birds before, let alone seen them...and where exactly was the Western Palaearctic?! They spoke casually of lesser rarities which seemed almost common on Scilly; birds such as Yellow-browed Warbler, Rose-coloured Starling and Red-breasted Flycatcher. I had never seen any of these either. I always seemed to be away on the very rare occasions that such rare and unusual birds were found in Christchurch; inevitably they had gone when I returned. Anyway I was sold: I had to go to Scilly. I had just finished reading Bill Oddie's *Little Black Bird Book*. I wanted this experience. I wanted to feel the excitement of seeing so many rare birds. I was determined to join the 1984 Choggers on their visit to Scilly, so when bookings were made in September my name was added to that of seven others.

Before leaving for Scilly I would need to be properly kitted out. True birders are never taken seriously without the proper gear. Top of the list comes a good pair of binoculars, or 'bins'. The ones I was using had suffered two near fatal accidents that had made them virtually useless. Periodically the prisms had to be realigned by giving them a judicious tap against a wall, a rock or the surface of the road. In the rain they also leaked and misted up badly. It needed an embarrassing amount of imagination to see birds others found with ease, and half the time there were twice as many as there should be.

One day in May in the pouring rain, a group of us had been searching the woods on Hengistbury Head for a reported Bonelli's Warbler. Rain dripped off the overhanging branches of oaks, plastering hair to scalp and causing unpleasant rivulets of water to trickle down our necks. My binoculars misted up both inside and out. I could see nothing, literally nothing at all. If all I could see on Scilly when a Scarlet Tanager put in an all too brief appearance was mist, my frustration would be hard to bear…so would the binoculars! I would probably throw them on the ground and jump up and down on them, or throw them into the sea.

A seasoned Scilly birder told me of a good 'value-for-money' pair of bins – Zeiss Jenoptems. I drove to Bournemouth to try to buy a pair. Could I get a pair? Could I hell!

"Jenoptems have been discontinued, Sir," said an assistant at a well-known camera shop. "We do have others which are just as good," he added helpfully. None of these were what I needed, or else they were far too expensive. Why does it always happen that a product that is cheap, efficient and popular is taken off the market just as one decides to buy it? I trudged from shop to shop. No good! Nothing! I cannot understand what had happened, because Jenoptems soon became readily available again. At long last I did find myself a similar, but considerably more expensive, pair in Winchester...so I had my bins. I decided not to buy myself an ornithological telescope (a 'scope to birders) yet. Although on Scilly, well-equipped birders load themselves up with scopes, tripods, bins and cameras wherever they go, I was told that when a rare bird is on view there are scopes by the hundred looking at it. There would usually be a birder on hand with a scope who would kindly let you have a quick look.

Next came clothes. First I bought myself a camouflaged combat jacket. Then having been told that the sea between the islands could get so rough that the open boats seem on the point of sinking with all hands, I bought myself a pair of waterproof trousers. Finally I needed the right footwear. Scilly birders do not wear wellies. A few wear trainers, but most use heavy climbing or walking boots. I was told of an excellent army surplus store where I could buy a pair of ex-German paratrooper's boots very reasonably. My mind began to dwell on the previous owner and how he might have come to part with them...anyway, off I went. I found myself in a dark little shop smelling faintly of cordite and leather. It was crammed with uniforms, medals, boots – the lot.

There was equipment relating to every conceivable army on this planet. In one corner a biker was choosing another iron cross for his jacket, while in another a skinhead was fingering a particularly ferocious looking knife. There were paratroopers' boots from all nations, even from countries one would scarcely imagine as having paratroopers. The most expensive were the German ones. I tried on a pair and found them surprisingly comfortable. I also bought some ex-army socks at 90 pence a pair. As I left the shop I hoped I was now more or less prepared for a fortnight's Scilly Birding.

Birders enjoying a rarity. Is this the attraction?

2. *The journey down*

October and the day of departure finally arrived. A young Chogger called Clive was giving me a lift down to Penzance. As we left, he mentioned that he had only just passed his driving test. This was to be his first long journey. When we left at six o'clock in the morning it was still dark, and I felt more than half-asleep. However, I was soon alert and full of apprehension. Clive's driving failed to reassure. As we sped seemingly out of control into the bends of Dorset and Devon, my heart was in my mouth. Perhaps I was not destined to see Scilly after all. I tried to quell my fear and raise my enthusiasm by talking to Clive about birds on Scilly. So far I had heard no reports of anything exciting on the islands. Could this be a bad year? I wasn't particularly worried as there would be plenty of lesser rarities to keep me going, and these I was certain to see according to Clive. As dawn began to break we approached Honiton. I know the roads quite well and was aware that we were approaching a particularly steep descent followed by a sharp right hand bend joining a major road.

"Clive", I said quietly, trying hard to stop my voice from trembling, "there's a nasty bend up ahead." In spite of my warning, we approached the bend at an alarming speed.

"Look out!" I shouted in abject fear and frustration at not being at the controls. Somehow or other we stayed on the road and unceremoniously entered Honiton. I was extremely relieved when we reached the easier, wider stretches of the dual carriageway that link Exeter and Plymouth. I began to daydream about American warblers, Nighthawks and Yellow-bellied Sapsuckers. I had been doing my homework before I left and at least knew what some of the American vagrants might look like. Was I really going to see some of these birds? It was a lovely thought.

Once into Cornwall, I began to notice birds and started a new list. A trip list for Scilly 1984. A Common Buzzard floated effortlessly on the thermals above the wooded valley of the Fowey. We passed Notter Bridge over the River Notter, Notter Garage and Indian Queens...strange names some places have in Cornwall! We passed Bodmin, and one or two Ravens with wedged tails tumbled acrobatically out of the sky. The weather deteriorated as we sped west. By the time we reached St. Ives, heavy rain was spattering the road and pavement from a leaden sky.

We saw a chap hitch-hiking with bins and a scope. We picked him up and took him to Penzance. As well as leaving a few twigs on the back seat of the car, he gave us a long list of birds that had been seen recently in the Scilly Isles. He was quite hard to understand as he had a strong local accent. Through it filtered Lesser Golden Plover, Yellowthroat and Swainson's Thrush – birds which to us had a special magic and mystique and which usually lived thousands of miles away. There were also no less than five Pectoral Sandpipers on the Drift Reservoir near Penzance. In conversation he told us he was travelling around Cornwall for the autumn, birding and sleeping rough.

The rain had eased a little by the time we reached Penzance. Before doing anything else, it was vital to book seats on the first available helicopter (known affectionately to Scilly birders as The Chopper). We arrived at the Airport and made enquiries at the desk. An attractive blonde girl wearing a British Airways uniform informed us apologetically.

"You're out of luck. No seats on any flights today, I'm afraid, Sir."

"What about tomorrow?" I asked anxiously.

"No. No seats on any flights tomorrow either", she replied. "You could always try standby. You'd be first in the queue if there are any cancellations."

"What are the chances?" I asked. "Fifty-fifty?" I added hopefully.

"I wouldn't say they were quite as good as that", she replied evasively. "There's no point in hanging around here at the moment. Come back and try again at two thirty and see if anyone's failed to turn up for the three ten."

It was now midday. We decided we would come back later and hope for cancellations. If we failed to get seats, we would have to look for a B&B somewhere and sail on the RMV *Scillonian III* in the early hours of next morning. That would involve a time-consuming sea crossing getting us to Scilly by midday. The sea can also be very rough. These were all good reasons for trying to get seats on the Chopper if at all possible. In any event, we had the best part of two hours to kill.

"Why not, let's go and try those peck sands at the Drift", I suggested. "We should just about have time. After all, it's not too far, is it?"

"Okay", he replied, and we were off. As we left, it took us about ten minutes to get back into the stream of traffic going towards Penzance. Eventually a gap appeared. Clive revved the car hard, the clutch slipped alarmingly as it first moved gently forward and then lurched violently across the road. I was beginning to wonder whether my suggestion had been wise. At least we had survived the journey all the way from Dorset to Cornwall, so the short drive to the Drift Reservoir oughtn't to present a major risk.

"You'll need a new clutch pretty soon if you carry on like that", I observed.

"Oh, that's alright", he replied airily. "I'll run this car into the ground or wear out the clutch. Then I'll flog it and buy a new one." At the rate he was going that was going to be sooner rather than later…I hoped for his sake he was rich.

The lanes to the Drift Reservoir are narrow and tortuous. We all but stalled on most of the hills, and roadside vegetation scratched the paintwork. Somehow we arrived at the Drift in one piece. As we got out of the car we were aware that a high wind was blowing, disturbing the surface of the water in front of us. The opposite bank of the reservoir looked steep and bleak. Small wavelets were breaking on a narrow strip of shingle shoreline – it looked most unsuitable for birds. Slowly we scanned this unlikely shore, but there were no birds to be seen. Two other birders arrived and parked. Before they set off, they informed us that the Pectoral Sandpipers were down the other end of the reservoir.

"How far?" I asked anxiously, thinking of the helicopter.

"About twenty minutes walk at most, so long as you get a move on." They replied and set off. I donned my paratrooper's boots for the first time in earnest, and we set off too. On the way there we met one or two birders returning.

"Are they still there?" I enquired.

"No problem", they smiled. "Yes, they're still there. Look for an obvious log, and you should see them crouching in front of it." I thanked them, and watched them walking happily along the reservoir shore back towards their car.

When we arrived, the two birders who had arrived shortly after us hadn't seen anything; they were still scanning hard. This part of the reservoir looked much more promising. In front of us were a series of muddy creeks and inlets. The trouble was that the mud was covered in thick vegetation. Birds like Pectoral Sandpipers with good camouflage could hide in amongst the sedges and reeds and be very difficult to find. As if that weren't enough, there was a plethora of logs lying on the mud and on the edge of the creeks. Unless the birds obliged by moving out into the open, the search would be like looking for the proverbial needle in a haystack.

A Meadow Pipit evoked an excited "Ah!" from me after which I cringed in embarrassment. Meanwhile, one of the other birders had moved a few yards away from us. Moments later he signalled to us frantically, indicating that he had found the birds and that we should approach with extreme caution. This could well mean they were excitingly close. We were soon crouching beside him, and he pointed at a log straight in front of us. The birds were indeed beside a very large log. In fact, the log itself had been blocking our view of them from the position we had started our search. From where we now were, we could still approach them even closer, and, taking great care, we enjoyed excellent views. The birds were strutting backwards and forwards across the mud. From time to time they would hesitate for a moment or two, then prod the mud with beaks like pneumatic drills. The streaky pectoral patches on the breast and yellowish green legs were perfectly clear. I had seen just one Pectoral Sandpiper before, so these birds weren't lifers for me. They weren't even a year tick because I had had one as a lifer a fortnight ago at Rutland Reservoir. In any case, these were truly excellent views that the birds were giving us, and there were two of them. They were very enjoyable, and a most auspicious start to the trip.

However exciting watching these delightful birds might be, time was passing. We had a date with a chopper, which might or might not have spare seats for us. After stalling, over revving and flooding the engine of his car, Clive finally managed to get us under way again. We drove back to Penzance and the heliport. I gave a large sigh of relief when Clive parked the car and paid the parking fee. Inside the terminal building an ominously large number of people was already hanging about. We still had to wait three quarters of an hour before the next flight was due to leave. The attractive blonde girl in the ticket office told us that about ten minutes before the flight was due to leave she would be able to consider us. Evidently, the helicopter had space for twenty-four passengers; I had already counted sixteen. More people arrived with tickets, and their luggage was checked. They went and, looking smug, sat down in the departure lounge. It was dangerously close to the flight time when a familiar and more than slightly battered car rattled its way into the car park. Out of it stepped two fellow Choggers; the bearded, large-framed figure of Chris and his girlfriend Tessa. They were two old stagers having enjoyed Scilly birding for many years. Doing a quick count, I now reckoned there were twenty-four passengers booked in for the ten past three flight.

"Have you got tickets, Chris?" I asked with some degree of concern.

"Yeah, of course we have", he chuckled. "Haven't you?" I shook my head.

"Never mind, you'll get on", he smiled reassuringly. I'm afraid I didn't share his optimism. I felt green with envy. Why the hell hadn't we had the good sense to reserve seats, I asked myself. The answer was quite simple. Clive and I hadn't had the confidence to predict our arrival time in Penzance. Anyway, Chris and Tessa were late, so we helped them into the heliport with their luggage.

"Any seats left on this flight?", I asked as the stewardess behind the counter checked Chris and Tessa in. I fully expected her reply to be, "I'm sorry, Sir. Your friends have just completed our compliment for this flight. Still, you might be luckier with the next." In fact what she said was:

"It's looking good. There are still four seats to spare. I'll just check to make absolutely sure, and, if nobody else has arrived, you can check in." I could have hugged her. No one else came, so we bought tickets, checked ourselves and our stuff in and went to join Chris and Tessa in the departure lounge. The lounge was much more like a local bus depot than the departure area of an airport.

The four seats, which had been unclaimed, puzzled me. Chris explained that in October birders book seats in case something good turns up on Scilly. If there were nothing special, there would always be standby passengers like Clive and myself to take them up, so British Airways don't seem to mind. I had never been on a helicopter before. Boarding it was an ear-splitting business. The rotors were cleaving the air lethally less than six feet above my head. These rotors could take off somebody's head with ease I thought as I hurried past underneath them. The passenger cabin was very like that in any ordinary aircraft, if a great deal smaller. The stewardess went through the emergency drill as we taxied round to our take off point. It was hard to remember we were in a helicopter and not a small airliner.

The need to taxi puzzled me. Later I learned that this was for safety just in case anything went wrong. A helicopter, once airborne, could cause havoc and endanger lives in the departure lounge if, heaven forbid, it went out of control for any reason. After we had taxied for a hundred yards or so, the pilot seemed satisfied with our position, and we stopped moving over the grass. There was a sudden mighty roar from the engines, then, at first very slowly and gently, we became airborne. It was rather like going up in a lift. Soon we began to gain height more rapidly. Below us Penzance and the *Scillonian*, moored against the quay, fell away. Once at the required height, we flew out along the coast of Penwith.

"Look, there's a flock of Golden Plover…look, down there!" I shouted as we drifted over St. Just Airport. "And yes…yes, look. I can just make it out. There's a Lesser amongst them." In those days, Lesser Golden Plover had yet to be split into American and Pacific Golden Plovers. The two races were dealt with together under the single species Lesser Golden Plover. Of course, I could see nothing of the sort, but Chris and Tessa had told us they had spent the morning searching the area around St. Just airport for a reported Lesser Golden Plover. The difference between a Lesser and a Greater Golden Plover is extremely difficult, even with the aid of a powerful telescope. Chris grunted his disapproval at my childlike sense of humour.

Very soon Land's End and Cape Cornwall passed beneath us. We could see brown jagged rocks set in a deep azure sea ringed with white breakers. It was now a glorious sunny afternoon as we flew out over the sea. Spray-flecked waves a thousand feet below us contrasted with the dark blue of the sea. Occasionally, we could make out a trawler being buffeted by the heavy Atlantic swell. Although I pride myself on being a reasonably good sailor, I never like to push my luck. Seeing those waves made me very grateful that I was on the helicopter with no prospect of the *Scillonian* early next morning.

We could just about make out mature Gannets as they flew between the waves below us, snow white specks gleaming in the afternoon sun, contrasting with the deep blue grey of the sea. Little black birds like Storm Petrel or Manx Shearwater would have been quite impossible to see, but had a killer whale or dolphin swum beneath us, I am sure we would have had no problem seeing them.

Soon the island of St. Martin's with its accompanying reefs and cliffs bathed in surf appeared to our right. We lost height and came into land over the lichen-covered cliffs of St. Mary's. We climbed out of the helicopter and stood on a strip of tarmac surrounded by acres of windswept grass. So this was Scilly and the famous St. Mary's Airport, where so many rare birds had been seen. We had arrived safely. The rhythmic, ear-splitting whine of the helicopter blades made concentration difficult. While we waited for our luggage to be unloaded, I scanned the vast expanse of the airport for birds but could see nothing special. We all squeezed with our luggage into a waiting minibus which whisked us along leafy lanes to Hugh Town and up to the Garrison. This was to be our home for the next fortnight. It is called the Garrison because of its surrounding fortifications. The Garrison is almost an island connected to the rest of St. Mary's by a narrow strip of land on which sits much of Hugh Town. The road to the Garrison leaves Hugh Town by a narrow archway called the Sally Port, and the archway is only just wide enough for a minibus. Somehow all minibus drivers take it with confidence and panache. Beyond the archway, a steep hill rises past a fortification to playing fields and Greystones, the name of our bungalow, situated on the far side. Many is the time that I have struggled on weary, leaden legs up that hill after a successful day's birding, wishing we were more centrally placed.

When we had arrived at Greystones we had a quick look around and checked the groceries that our landlady had kindly left for us. Then, with almost indecent haste, we changed into our birding gear and were off.

On the boat to St. Agnes

3. First impressions of Scilly – and some good birds

"We're in Scilly", said Chris. Invisible antennae seemed to appear and sense the scene. "Where are the birders? Where are all the birders with all the gen?" We ambled off down the hill towards Hugh Town. Chris's sixth birding sense slowly homed in on what was about. "Let's go and look at Lower Moors", he announced suddenly and decisively. Lower Moors is an area of reed beds and scrubby willows and there is a pathway running right through it. Half way along, a birder's hide looks out onto a very promising lagoon. It was from this path that I was soon going to have my first taste of Scilly birding. We caught up with a stationery group of about fifteen birders.

"What do you reckon they've got?" I asked.

"There was an Icky (Icterine Warbler) here earlier", said Chris with about as much enthusiasm and emotion as he might have said 'starling'.

"An Icky! Great!" I enthused, scarcely able to control my excitement. An Icky was a full lifer tick as far as I was concerned, and this was after only half an hour's birding. This was incredible! We stood still and watched in silence. To my utter astonishment and delight, after just five minutes Tessa whispered softly.

"I've got it…in the hedge…just above the post, and beyond the highest bit. It's sitting on a paler branch, which is about halfway down. There! Oh! It's hopping left." Sure enough, there it was, a little grey warbler with a rather domed head. This was a particularly pleasing Icky as it had well-marked, paler wing panels, and these are one of the best identification features of Icterine Warblers. An Icky is a member of the *Hippolais* group of warblers, known as hippos amongst birders. No *Hippolais* warbler breeds in Britain, and none are often seen. Apart from hearing a Melodious Warbler singing in Spain, this was my first hippo...it was all seeming astonishingly easy.

"Cor an Icky...and the first lifer of the trip UTB (under the belt) already", I bubbled with enthusiasm. At that moment I didn't know it, but about ten minutes later I would be having my second.

Along a lane about a hundred yards from the Icterine Warbler, we came across another small group of birders craning to catch a glimpse of something in the top of an oak tree. The bird of the moment here was a Yellow-browed Warbler. Small birds hopped and flitted amongst the leaves above us, but as we arrived they were all either Chiffchaffs or Blue Tits. At this stage of the trip patience was not my strong point. The five minutes or so before someone announced, "There it is...it's...it's up there on the left...ach, it's flown left", seemed an eternity. I did see the bird fly, but it was an unidentifiable blur of grey. It was another five minutes before someone else caught up with it on the lower branch of an apple tree a few yards further on. I moved up to the spot and caught up with it properly. What an utterly delightful little bird it turned out to be. It looked like a cross between a Willow Warbler and a Goldcrest without the golden crown stripe. The two yellow wing bars and supercilium (paler stripe above the eye) left me in no doubt that the bird I had seen was indeed a Yellow-browed Warbler. It was a second very pleasing lifer tick in a surprisingly short time, and the entertainment that afternoon was still not yet quite finished.

Gradually, as we walked around the island and the light began to fade, we picked up the available gen. There had been a Red-necked Grebe in a nearby bay, but it wasn't there when we looked. We heard of a Rough-legged Buzzard, which was popping up all over the place; it seemed it could turn up almost anywhere. Earlier that day, it had actually been seen flying up Hugh Town High Street! The most likely spot to see it, according to available gen, seemed to be on certain rocks just off shore. We scanned the coast just in case but couldn't see it. Dusk began to settle over the misty blue grey waters of the Scilly Roads, the stretch of sea which separates St. Mary's from Tresco, Bryher and Samson. We made our way back to Hugh Town and enjoyed supper, several beers and much bird conversation at a very good pub called the Mermaid.

Suddenly, as dusk darkened the sky, out of the blue Chris shouted, "There's the Rough-legged Buzzard!"

"Where!" I demanded excitedly.

"Up there", he replied, pointing up at an alcove above a shop doorway where a bird of prey, carved in wood, sat surveying the scene.

That evening, after supper and several pints in the Mermaid, I was introduced to one of the most important establishments for birders in Scilly in those days, the Porthcressa or 'Cressa as it was known affectionately amongst the Scilly birding fraternity, the nerve centre of the Scilly Birding population. In 1984, two people were responsible for running it, having made it what it was. They were Mike Rogers and David Hunt. Sadly, shortly after the 1984 Scilly season, David Hunt was killed by a tiger while leading a birding trip in India. He was then the owner of the Porthcressa, which has changed quite a bit since. The Porthcressa was a café by day, but at night a large cellar bar opened below. This was where the birders congregated in the evenings. After a hard day's birding, large quantities of beer were consumed and adventures told, retold and more often than not embroidered.

At nine o'clock sharp, Mike Rogers would take centre stage. In front of him in a dark, smoke filled auditorium sat rows of eager birders. It was time for the Scilly Bird Log. It was rather like a cross between bingo, an auction of antiques in a local village hall and stand-up comedy in a northern working men's club. Everything would go quiet. Mike Rogers would move to the microphone and, after a few pleasantries, start to call out the names of birds. Birders would then call out the numbers of each species and the sites they had seen them at during the day.

On this occasion, we had lingered over our meal in the Mermaid and were late. We didn't manage to get a seat and spent the session squashed up against the bar. All we could see of Mike Rogers was a strangely disconnected reflection in a mirror on the wall opposite. The image was misty and slightly distorted; arms waved in the air as if they were conducting a symphony orchestra, but for us the 'orchestra' was facing in the wrong direction. We could clearly hear the amplified voice of Mike Rogers but nothing of the audience. It was very clipped, disconnected, and went something like this:

"Stonechat. Okay Mary's?... two P'thellick, two Lower Moors, any more?... One Garrison... Is that all?... Where have they gone! Other islands, Aggie?... Tresco?... None on Tresco? Well I saw one near Abbey Pool. Everyone's too busy concentrating on Dusky Warblers on Tresco today it seems. (Laughter)... Ah, two Old Grimsby, that's better. Martin's... hardly worth asking. No one goes to Martin's, do they? It'll be your fault if a really good Yankee turns up there and nobody sees it... Ah, two Martin's. So birders do go to Martin's occasionally; Bryher?" ... Silence.

So it went on, very staccato, but with some extraordinarily clever repartee carefully interlaced with the latest birders' jargon. Up-to-the-minute bird publications were displayed on a trestle table and sold at the Porthcressa. Each evening after the log there was an illustrated talk on the inevitable subject of birds. Talks were given by real celebrities. These were people such as the late P. J. Grant, author of his magnificent gull guide and co-author of many other excellent bird books, or perhaps Richard Millington. In those days, he was known mainly for being a bird artist and as the author of *A Twitcher's Diary*. Little did we know what was in his mind at that time. Within a year or two, he and several birding colleagues would have organised *Birdline* and the excellent monthly magazine *Birding World*. It is strange to think that in 1984 *Birdline* was still a thing of the future. In those days we still had to rely on the grapevine centred on Nancy's, a small café at Cley in Norfolk, close to the nerve centre of mainland birding. A telephone line in the café was manned virtually twenty-four hours, and birders could get the latest gen.

Another contributor to the evening might be Ron Johns. In those days his British life list was undisputedly the longest. Since then his long, unchallenged supremacy has been toppled by birders such as Lee Evans. Ron Johns actually appeared in the *Guinness Book of Records* as having the longest British bird list! On the wall there was a table showing the current British lifer scores with Ron John's name at the top. Several years on, the best British life lists top 500 birds, but in those days Ron Johns' 460 seemed an unassailable score. My life list now stands at something like 415, but at that time I was very proud of my meagre 279, which it reached after the 1984 Scilly Season.

By day, when the Porthcressa reverted to being a café, its image changed completely. Downstairs the bar was shut. As a café it dispensed mugs of tea, coffee and hospitality, as well as plates of pie, chips and beans to passing hungry birders. Birders with tired legs, having traipsed around the island, would come to relax and chat. They would grip one another off and tell yarns with glazed expressions on their faces in fond recollection of the latest crippler. It was also the nerve centre for all birding activities on the islands. The headquarters of 'Radio Birdbrain' was concealed in a secluded corner. This was the brainchild of the late David Hunt. In 1984, throughout October, a network of CB radios covered the Scilly Isles. These reported back to Radio Birdbrain with the latest gen. As the information came in, it was written up on a board outside the Porthcressa and transmitted to similar boards in other parts of the islands. Reports appeared in a variety of coloured chalk in an attempt to highlight birds of particular importance.

A typical announcement might have read as follows:

Yellowthroat   *7.30 Bryher...not since*
R B Fly   *2 Garrison in pines*
Barred Warb   *Garrison*
Dick's Pip   *1 Golf Co*
Lap Bunt   *2 P'hellick*
Swainson's   *Not yet today*

Before ten o'clock in the morning, the board often announced 'No news is bad news, so go out and make news.' On one occasion at least, this caption remained on the board all day. When this happened, things were described depressingly as 'quiet'. As a result of this highly efficient system, the birders, the islands and most important the boatmen were kept up to date with "What's about". Each boat going to the other islands had its own CB radio, and the boatmen were highly competitive in their pursuit of the lucrative birders' trade. It was not unknown for a boat bound for, say Tresco, to be turned back to St.

Mary's as a better bird had just been turned up there. Generally a vote was taken and, if a return was indicated, those who still wanted to go on had to wait.

The boatmen are excellent and very patient with the demands of the birders. They usually know which birds will cause a stir, and therefore bring them good trade; however, I doubt if more than a handful would actually recognise the birds if they saw them. Sometimes they will risk dangerous tides, rough seas and difficult landings to get birders within ticking distance of their birds. Wicked thoughts concerning boatmen have occasionally been voiced, but I am utterly certain there is no truth in these rumours. Boatmen have been accused of flying to the United States with mist nets...need I say more!

After we had left the Porthcressa that first evening and returned to Greystones, we discussed plans for the following day. From the available gen, the situation in the islands was as follows:

? Common Yellowthroat   *Bryher – but not seen recently.*
(This was a very desirable American warbler making its second appearance ever in the British Isles.)
Rough-legged Buzzard   *Here, there and everywhere*
1+ Lapland Bunting   *St. Mary's Golf Course*
Dotterel   *the Airport*
Blackpoll Warbler   *St. Agnes*
(Another desirable American warbler, but with several more British appearances to its credit.)
Wryneck
Wood Warbler
Red-necked Grebe
Corncrake
Bluethroat   *St. Agnes*

Now that apparently the Yellowthroat had gone, the opinion of Chris and Tessa, which was backed up by the rest of us, was that there was only one real crippler on the Scillies, and that was the Blackpoll Warbler which had taken up residence on St. Agnes.

"What on earth is a 'crippler'?" I asked myself but, not wanting to display my ignorance, kept silent. My first thoughts concerning the birding accolade crippler were that it must be reserved for birds so difficult to find that people literally crippled themselves in their attempts to find them. I was wrong. A bird that gains the exalted status of crippler is one which is so desirable and wonderful that views of it cripple the observer. Excellent views of a crippler are therefore described as crippling views!

Evidently, according to the latest gen, this particular Blackpoll Warbler wasn't giving crippling views to anyone. The only available information was that it had put in an all too brief appearance on a particular row of runner beans on a vegetable patch opposite St. Agnes Post Office. Last time this happened, it was within a minute or two of half past twelve.

"This bird isn't properly sussed yet", Tessa observed. "We may have to wait a bit until its movements are better known."

"Where is it for the rest of the time?" I asked naively.
"In other fields, allotments...who knows? It could be anywhere", Chris added helpfully.

"Why don't people go out and look for it then?" I asked.

"It's not quite that simple, Simon", Chris replied patiently. "You see, it's just not done. You can't go trampling over other people allotments and things without causing a great deal of bother and offence to the local residents. They just don't like it, see? We've simply got to wait until someone finds another place where this bird likes to be. At the moment, all we know is that the bird seems to like being on those runner beans at approximately twelve thirty. So if we want to see it, that's where we'd better be."

It was something that had never occurred to me, that birds might live by the clock, but when this fortnight on Scilly was over I had had many experiences which led me to believe that birds might lead very structured lives. So tomorrow it was to be St. Agnes for this Blackpoll Warbler. Lastly, we looked at the pictures in the *National Geographic Field Guide to the Birds of North American* to make sure we knew what we would be looking for.

4. Birds, birds...and more birds

After an excellent breakfast of bacon and eggs, the four of us left for the quay to catch the ten fifteen boat to St. Agnes. Before we left Greystones, we jotted down the latest gen for Brian who would be arriving later that afternoon. Brian is quite literally a giant of a bird watcher, being at least six foot five tall. He was also known affectionately as the 'Jolly Green Giant.'

It was on my way down to the boat that morning that I enjoyed my first view of the Scilly Roads from the Garrison. It is a wonderfully beautiful panorama. There before us lay the wide expanse of blue water which separates St. Mary's from the other islands. Tresco, Bryher and Samson could be seen in a line about two miles away, with St. Agnes almost completely obscured off to the left. Each island was surrounded by rocky coves and sandy beaches, the sand a brilliant creamy white against the blue of the sea. I don't think I could ever tire of this view. As my fortnight on Scilly progressed, so I was to see it in many moods from the misty soft blue of a fine, autumnal morning, through the fierce white and grey of a stormy day to the vivid red and gold of a brilliant sunset.

When we arrived at the quay, there were two boats crammed to the gunwales with Blackpoll Warbler twitchers. They were a Barbour-jacketed, grey-green mass of humanity, each clutching a telescope and with binoculars suspended from their necks. We had to wait for a third boat. A few people, mostly islanders, wanted to go to Tresco, so our boat would have to waste time going there first.

Before leaving for Scilly, I had been given some friendly advice on etiquette and survival as a Scilly birder. The most important rules, which everyone ought to obey if they wanted to retain their street cred, were as follows:

1. Never stare through binoculars or a telescope at a common bird for more than a second or two. If you do, you will rapidly attract a crowd who will start demanding, "What have you got?" or "What's the attraction?"

2. Never, never say, "I think I've found a crippler!" If it really is blatantly obvious what you've got, admit to a Hoopoe or a male Golden Oriole if you get excellent views, but never a Dusky or Arctic Warbler. The only time you may is if you have had crippling views, at leisure; you've taken full notes and made some nice drawings. You also need to be an ace birder with a reputation for accuracy and masses of confidence.

3. Keep a low profile. Don't start rumours! False rumours make for bad reputations on Scilly very rapidly, and bad reputations can be difficult to get rid of.

So, when we were approaching Tresco and I saw an interesting bird on the sea, I kept mum. When I had been watching it for less than five seconds, it dived. It looked like a Red-necked Grebe. Normally I would have shouted, "Look everybody, look! A Red-necked Grebe over there, look!" Unfortunately, I wasn't absolutely one hundred percent certain that, when it surfaced, it wouldn't by some strange and embarrassing quirk have miraculously transformed itself into a Shag. It surfaced again and I had a good look. A Red-necked Grebe was, after all, reportedly in the area, and the bird I could see certainly looked okay.

I whispered to my neighbour, "There's a Red-necked Grebe over there." He scanned where I had indicated, found the bird and agreed with me. It was too late to tell many others about it, as we had soon left it far behind. None of my friends saw it, but I think I was right to be cautious. An awful lot of birds will change dramatically after you have just announced a rarity to the world. This was also my first full day on Scilly, and I was still very conscious of how reputations could be made or destroyed. A few days later, close to the spot where I saw my Red-necked Grebe, a female Surf Scoter was seen by a boatload of birders on their way out to Tresco. By the time they were heading back to St. Mary's, it had been 'transformed' into a definite female Common Scoter.

Eventually, after the detour to Tresco, our boat moored at the landing stage on St. Agnes. About eighty eager birders leapt off the boat and shot off up the road at high speed. They were full of determination to see the Blackpoll Warbler as soon as possible. Our party held back. Evidently we weren't going to rush after this particular crippler. In any case it was only eleven o'clock, so there was no real panic yet. A couple of Redwing flew overhead calling, a nice bird for the time of year even if they were heralds of approaching winter. We scanned allotments and some birds moved around in the *Pittosporum*. *Pittosporum* (or 'Pitty' to a Scilly birder) is a foreign shrub which is well established on Scilly and is used extensively for hedging. It forms impenetrable thickets that provide excellent cover for flocks of foraging birds. However, none of the ones we could see foraging at that moment was a Blackpoll Warbler.

After wandering down the lane with remarkable sangfroid, we arrived at the vegetable patch opposite the post office. The latest gen told us we had been quite right not to rush; the bird hadn't been seen yet that morning by anyone. There in front of us, behind a low dry stone wall, was that famous row of runner beans. The allotment was rather small, wedge-shaped and surrounded on all sides, except for the roadside, by thick *Pittosporum*. By now it was midday, and there were a hundred birders at least staring intently at that row of runner beans. Our party joined the vigil.

I thought to myself that this is stupid. Everyone's far too close. No bird's going to come out onto those runner beans with us lot just eight yards away. This is just daft. On the other hand, an awful lot of birders do seem to think it's worth it, and they know much more about Scilly birding than I do. Perhaps birds in Scilly in the autumn do behave strangely. A House Sparrow hopped out of the *Pittosporum* and onto the ground in front of the beans. To my immediate left, a birder lifted his bins making suspicious rustling noises with his Barbour jacket. The

Waiting for the Blackpoll Warbler on St. Agnes

noise caused an immediate chorus of rustling as other birders joined in by raising their bins. Everyone was super alert and twitchy, and even the slightest movement or sound caused a rustle which would then cause ripples and rumours of muffled excitement. We all stood, all but immobilized, stared and rustled. Occasionally a rustle would cause someone to whisper excitedly, "Are you on it…is it there?" or "What's that up in the Pitty?"

There were two ways of raising binoculars, and I began to wonder whether they didn't contain subliminal messages. The first was fast and with a rustle. In this way the birder was indicating, without the potential embarrassment of actually saying anything, that he thought he was onto something. Secondly, binoculars could be raised slowly and casually, simply to alleviate boredom.

But even so it was a lovely day, the sun was shining; Scilly in October is a gorgeous, peaceful place to be. Deep philosophical thoughts might have been a good way of passing the time. The seconds ticked by inexorably towards the magic hour of twelve thirty. No one dared look at his or her watch for fear of causing a rustle. Sparrows, Wrens and Chiffchaffs began to arrive on the patch of soil in front of the *Pittosporum*, trying ever so hard to be cripplers. They executed feats of incredible acrobatic daring all over those wretched runner beans. They were all giving what could be described as absolute crippling views but, unfortunately for them and for us, none was a Blackpoll Warbler.

Suddenly, from the distance, the silence was broken by a muffled thump, thump, thump… which grew louder and louder. A wave of birding humanity in boot-clad feet was running up the road towards us. It then buried itself into a virtually impenetrable *Pittosporum* hedge above a most uncomfortable dry stone wall. We hurried to join them and managed to squeeze into the tiniest crevice still available in a solid wall of prone bodies. All we were rewarded with was a sea of virtually impenetrable vegetation.

Faintest whispers!

"Where is it?"

"Is anyone actually on it?"

"After all that I suppose it is actually out there somewhere."

I was in a desperately uncomfortable position and beginning to wonder how long I could stay staring into my particular gap without suffering the ravages of agonizing cramp.

"See that scarecrow", came the eventual reply to everyone's desperate enquiry. I could actually see the scarecrow through a tiny chink in the vegetation in front of me. "It's at eleven o'clock from the scarecrow's nose, eating caterpillars on the top of a cabbage." And sure enough, there it was – a streaky little warbler. Suddenly it dived towards other cabbages and out of my view to the left.

"Oh shit…who's on it?…is anybody on it still?"

"Ooooh, what a fantastic, amazing little bird…Oh shit!!!"

"Where's it gone…is anyone actually on it now?"

Much to the annoyance of those who had yet to see it, which appeared to be most, the bird had moved on. It was probably in another corner of the same field but out of sight to any birder, so no one was actually on it. Well, I had seen the Blackpoll Warbler. Hardly crippling views, but quite enough to realise it corresponded to the little bird we had been studying in the American guide. Even though the views weren't crippling, I had seen my first American passerine which was now safely on my list and I felt a very pleasant, warm glow of satisfaction flow through me. I decided I was definitely into this Scilly birding business. This Blackpoll Warbler, I had been assured, was going to be difficult to catch up with – and I had seen it. I decided to move away and give somebody else a chance. In any case, my left arm and right calf muscle were beginning to ache unbearably with the unnatural position I was in. It was a relief to stand upright again. I caught site of Tessa.

"Did you see it?" I asked.

"Yeah", she replied. "But I don't think Chris did."

Moments later Chris appeared looking far from amused.

"I'm not getting down on my hands and knees for any damn bird", he spat angrily when Tessa suggested he might just have room to squeeze between two frantic, prone bodies. I decided to move on. I had seen the bird, and I didn't think I was going to get better views unless it turned up somewhere else. Suddenly out of nowhere a breathless birder appeared and shouted.

"Rough-legged Buzzard!"

"Where?"

"Up towards the Turk's Head."

"Great!" So we all took more exercise as we thumped our way back up the hill towards the local pub and the landing stage. The Rough-legged Buzzard took appreciable pressure off those who still hadn't seen the Blackpoll Warbler. For some, it simply alleviated the frustration by giving them something else to do. I arrived at the top of the hill to catch a glimpse of a bird of prey flying off into the distance towards the other end of the island. I just had time to gasp a question to Chris and Tessa,

"Get better views of the Blackpoll?" They had just arrived on the scene as I started legging it back as fast as I could in the direction I had just come. I arrived at the other end of the island to be told that the bird had disappeared into a bush on the shore.

"Seen the Firecrest in the Parsonage?" asked the chap who

had just told me where the Rough-legged Buzzard had gone.

"Where's the Parsonage?" I asked.

"Go back down towards the Post Office and just before you get there, turn left and it's a hundred yards down on your right." I thanked him. A Firecrest would have been nice, but I glanced at my watch. Amazingly it was still a few minutes before twelve thirty, the magical time when the Blackpoll Warbler was reputed to put in its appearance on the runner beans. As better views of that would be far more important than any Firecrest, I walked briskly down to the Post Office again.

To my great surprise when I arrived there, the area in front of the runner beans was deserted. However, there was a sea of abandoned telescopes all pointing towards them; an amazing sight! I was so amused I took a photograph before strolling up towards the main Blackpoll Warbler scrum. This was still embedded in the *Pittosporum* above the dry stone wall. I listened to the latest gen.

"It's crossed the road and should be moving down towards the runner bean patch. In fact, it ought to be there any minute."

Chris and Tessa were side by side looking through quite a generous gap which they had to themselves on the opposite side of the road. Their demeanour seemed to suggest that they were onto something, so I joined them. There in front of us in a clearing full of cabbages was the Blackpoll Warbler busily collecting caterpillars. It was extremely close. These were much better views, less frantic and in far greater comfort. After a minute or two of sheer birding pleasure the bird flew off and out of site. A much happier Chris left the gap, stood up, stretched and smiled.

"That was nice", he beamed. "Thank God for that. For a moment I thought I might have to come back here again tomorrow for more suffering." We strolled off towards the Turk's Head where we were looking forward to enjoying a celebratory pint and a pasty. Within seconds a messenger in the guise of a breathless and excited birder came rushing up the hill towards us.

"Semi-p's turned up on Tresco", he gasped. "The experts have confirmed it, so it's gen. Boat's leaving for Tresco in quarter of an hour."

"What on earth's a Semi-p?" I asked the others.

"It's a Semi-palmated Sandpiper – an American wader which looks remarkably similar to a Little Stint", Chris replied informatively. If I were to see it, it would be yet another lifer. If I were to count the Rough-legged Buzzard, it would be three in a day. This was utter magic...quite incredible. I had been on Scilly for less than twenty-four hours, and new birds were coming in thick and fast.

"What do you reckon", I asked, trying desperately hard to curb my bubbling enthusiasm and considerable anxiety.

"Yeah, might as well give it a whirl", Chris smiled phlegmatically. How on earth could he be so calm? Perhaps he had already had a Semi-p. We scarcely had time to burn our mouths with piping hot pasties in the Turk's Head, then attempt to soothe our palates with a rushed pint before heading off to the quay. Clive remained behind on St. Agnes as he had yet to see the Blackpoll Warbler to his satisfaction.

As the boat slid across the water towards Tresco, a young birder asked his companion earnestly how many American peeps he had had. What on earth is a peep? I asked myself. It turns out that the Americans call small, stint-sized waders peeps. So here we were, a group of supposedly sane adults sitting in a boat bound for Tresco with the sole intention of ticking a peep! The mind boggles!

A soon as the boat touched the quay on Tresco, eager birders scrambled off in a desperate wave in the direction of the interior. They belted off down the road like a herd of buffalo and were soon lost over the horizon. Much to my frustration, Chris, Tessa and I ambled along. We strolled across the strip of heathland in the general direction of the Great Pool, which was where the Semi-p had been reported.

By now it was very warm, and a strong sun shone from a cloudless blue sky. We crossed the helicopter pad on the far side of the heath and walked into the Abbey Gardens. It was October and they were past their best but still retained their tropical atmosphere. There were yuccas overhung by great branching palms. Pink Jersey and Guernsey Lilies tried not to be outdone by the blue of *Agapanthus* flowers. The Scillies are renowned for their bulbs. Many of them, though scarcely frost hardy, have become thoroughly established in Scilly because of the mild climate. They still look out of place when growing beside more everyday plants such as bracken.

A familiar sound brought me back to earth. It came from a nearby *Pittosporum* hedge.

"That's familiar. What the hell is it?" I asked. A bright green Budgerigar flew out of the bush, answering my question as well as adding to the exotic nature of the scene.

Eventually we arrived on the shores of Abbey Pool. On the opposite shore was a line of birders behind a row of telescopes. Abbey Pool and Great Pool on Tresco are the largest bodies of open water in the Scillies and are usually the best sites for waders and wild-fowl.

In 1984, a Black Duck, a species of American wildfowl, had only recently departed from Great Pool where it had taken up residence for several years. It was sad that it wasn't still there for me in 1984, but a local male Mallard must have fancied her because she certainly left her mark on her hybrid offspring, no doubt, for generations to come. In the 1990s, a drake male took her place, and that constituted my Black Duck tick. At the time, I thought it was a pity that it was not considered ethical to tick a hybrid any more than it was ethical to tick a Budgerigar, however at home it might seem in the Abbey Gardens. I found out later that some consider the Golden Pheasants in the Abbey Gardens to be sufficiently well established to be tickable. Yet, on this particular afternoon, in spite of our apparent laid-back approach, we were supposed to be after a Semi-palmated Sandpiper. I became a little worried when I noticed that the birders on the other side of the lake weren't looking through either binoculars or telescopes. Others were walking away aimlessly. Had it gone? Surely not! We went round to the other side of the lake and joined the small group of birders who were left. They told us that the Semi-palmated Sandpiper was flying with a group of about a dozen Dunlin to various parts of the lakeshore. They were settling and feeding for a few moments before moving off to another spot. We didn't have to wait very long before the little party plopped itself down on the shore very close to us. I scanned the flock and could see that amongst the Dunlins was a bird which was noticeably smaller, with a shorter, straighter beak. It looked exactly like a Little Stint. Since no Little Stint had been reported, I supposed that this had to be the bird of the moment.

"Chris."

"Yes?"

"Er...why isn't it a Little Stint?" I asked. At first, Chris simply pretended not to hear me.

"Chris," I persisted. "It looks ever so like a Little Stint to me. Why isn't it?"

You see, having got this little bird in front of me, I was

rather keen to be able to see exactly why it was a Semi-palmated Sandpiper. A little later I found out that Chris would have liked to have known what its distinguishing features were too. He was quietly cursing me because he couldn't give me a satisfactory answer, and my questioning was being very public.

"Well it's um...it's got semi-palmations, hasn't it?" he replied lamely, hoping this would shut me up. Semi-palmations, from which the bird gets its name, are very slight webbing between the toes. The bird was busily trotting backwards and forwards very fast, just like a Little Stint. Even during the brief moments it stood still, when its feet were more often than not covered in water, I certainly couldn't make out the semi-palmations. Later on, on the boat back to St. Mary's, some eager young lads were earnestly discussing the matter.

"The semi-palmations may have been difficult to see", they conceded. "But there was absolutely no sign of any braces, and the lower mandible was really obvious. The beak was a totally different shape. Frankly it couldn't have been anything but a Semi-p...I really don't know what all the discussion and fuss was all about." It will be a red-letter day, if ever it comes when I have that sort of confidence. However, I had had excellent views of the bird in question, and if the experts said it was a Semi-palmated Sandpiper that would have to be good enough for me.

We were making our way slowly back to the boat when someone within earshot mentioned a Grey Phalarope. A Grey Phalarope is another wader but very different in character from the Semi-p. They feed by swimming in tight, frantic circles, stirring up aquatic insects and crustaceans, darting about and jabbing at the water with their longish beaks. More often than not, they seem almost oblivious of humans. Once I saw a photographer having to move away from a Red-necked Phalarope because it was moving too close to him for him to focus on it with his telephoto lens. This particular phalarope was also nice and close, and Chris took several photos. In fact, it was a rather nice bird as it still had a trace of summer-plumage red on its throat.

Having enjoyed the phalarope, we walked slowly towards the boat.

"There's a probable Melodious Warbler at Little Grimsby by the Island Hotel," a passing birder informed us excitedly.

"How about it?" I asked enthusiastically. "We've just about got time."

"Melodious isn't a mega problem", Chris replied dismissively. "They're pretty regular. I should forget it, especially as it's only a probable. You're bound to catch up with one sooner or later." I didn't quite share his confidence. When people assure you that birds you haven't seen are easy, and I had only heard a Melodious Warbler in Spain, they have an irritating habit of developing into bogey birds.

On arrival at the boat, we collapsed gratefully into the seats. We were all feeling hot and tired after an amazing, but physically demanding day. It seemed ages since we had set off for St. Agnes. In true birding tradition, we were dressed in anoraks, combat or Barbour jackets, with pullovers tied around our wastes, and our legs were weighed down by heavy boots.

The last bird of that day on Tresco scarcely caused any attention at all. As the boat pulled away from the quay to return to St. Mary's, two Ravens flew overhead. As there were only three Ravens resident in Scilly at the time, this was quite an unusual sighting. We were so tired we hardly gave them a second glance.

Although it had been a truly memorable and amazing day, things were about to go wrong for me. I was about to experience a Scilly sensation for the first time, and this would be far from pleasant. I was about to be gripped off! The grip off I was to experience was far less unpleasant than it could have been. It wasn't half as painful as a grip off another member of our party was going to get later on.

A grip off occurs when a birder sees a bird which a second birder particularly wants to see. The bird may be particularly difficult to catch up with, and the gripped-off birder may have already wasted hours trying to catch up with it. By the time the second birder hears of the bird and is gripped off, it is either too dark or the bird has flown off never to be seen again. The one gripped off has made a wrong decision, and he knows it. He has been in the wrong place at the wrong time.

I met a young birder once who said he felt physically sick if he ever dipped on an important bird. A birder dips on a bird if he fails to see the bird he's after. This lad would have made a prime target for a grip off. But in his case it would have been rather unkind and very unwise. He would probably have been sick, quite literally!

In many ways I deserved to be gripped off when I stepped off that boat from Tresco. There were two potential lifers left for me that day on St. Mary's. I had already enjoyed three lifer ticks that day. To expect five in one day was perhaps just a little bit greedy! The potential lifer tick birds were Lapland Bunting and Dotterel. Both had been seen that morning on St. Mary's Golf Course. The Dotterel had been around for a day or two and had also been seen up on the airport. Chris suggested that I take a look at the golf course through my binoculars as we approached St. Mary's quay. If there were crowds of birders up there, the chances were I'd be lucky, he explained. Unfortunately, I could see that there was scarcely anyone there. I could just about make out the odd dog walker, but there was certainly no crowd of birdwatchers. In spite of this, I shot off towards the golf course at high speed as soon as the boat was tied to the quay. It was one and a half miles at least, and it had been a long day already. The last stretch is up a steep incline. As I arrived I met one or two birders ambling casually in the opposite direction.

"Any news on the Lapland?" I panted.

"Not recently", one of them replied. "It hasn't been seen since early morning, at least not on the golf course. I suppose it could be skulking in the rough, but everyone's been having a pretty good look." I thanked them but, in spite of what they had said, thought I might just as well give it a go now that I'd got there. On the golf course were one or two golfers trying to play golf, while a few birders were still trying to find birds. Birders do, at least mostly, keep to the edge, trying not to interfere with play.

It soon became apparent that attempting to find that Lapland Bunting was probably worse than looking for the proverbial needle in a haystack. At least the proverbial needle is in the haystack, but it soon became evident that the Lapland Bunting was almost certainly not even on the golf course.

I got into conversation with a fellow birder who came from Andover. We could see the airport easily from where we were. As it only looked a couple of hundred yards away, I suggested we try over there. It may have only looked that close, but there is a deep valley between the golf course and the airport, and in the end it certainly felt like the couple of miles it turned out to be on the map. When eventually we did arrive, all we could find were three Golden Plover, and there wasn't even a Lesser with them to brighten up the evening. Reluctantly we decided to give up and headed back to town. As we walked along the cliffs, we watched the last rays of a brilliant red sunset merging with the mists hanging over St. Agnes in the distance. It had been an amazing day. After all Lapland Bunting and Dotterel were not that rare, and I was pretty certain I would catch up with them before too long.

As I made my weary way up towards the Garrison I met the unmistakable figure of the Jolly Green Giant coming the other way.

"Hello Simon, how's tricks?" he greeted me cheerfully with a smile.

"Great", I replied. "How are things with you? Seen anything yet?" I asked automatically.

"There's a couple of Yellow-browed Warblers and a Barred Warbler on the Garrison", he replied.

"Where's the Barred Warbler?" I demanded eagerly. Barred Warbler would have been another tick.

"Round beyond the crowd trying to get to grips with the Yellow-browed's", he replied. "But it's getting a bit gloomy for it now, isn't it? I'd wait and give it a go in the morning if I were you." I knew he was right. Reluctantly I joined him, and we walked together back to Greystones where I found Chris and Tessa sitting back and enjoying a refreshing cup of tea.

"How'd you get on", Chris asked, a broad grin on his face knowing precisely what I was going to say.

"I've just walked a hell of a long way", I replied. "And my feet feel like raw liver. First I struggled up to the golf course."

"It wasn't there, was it?" Chris smiled. He was enjoying himself. "I told you it wouldn't be, but you wouldn't listen."

"After that, being a glutton for punishment, I struggled across to the airport where I saw three Golden Plovers and not a lot else." I eased my aching feet out of the boots. Chris was still smiling his wretched head off.

"I've heard about the Barred Warbler on the Garrison by the way", I announced tersely. Chris was still smiling, and I could feel a potential grip off beginning to take hold. "You didn't see anything else, did you?" I asked casually, dreading the answer.

"Couple of RB Flickers on the Garrison!" Chris smiled casually.

"RB Flickers...what are they?" I asked anxiously.

"Red-breasted Flycatchers!" Chris answered triumphantly. Chris knew how much I wanted to see this species. It was a bogey bird which I had failed to see on several occasions. It was close to the top of my Scilly shopping list! The grip off was complete.

"Hell, hell, hell!" I exclaimed. "You're having me on...you didn't really, did you? And you saw two of them. You saw the Barred Warbler as well, I suppose."

"Oh yes, we saw that brilliantly." Chris was still smiling. "We had brilliant views of that, but it was those little white markings on the tails of the RB Flickers that we really enjoyed."

"Hell and damnation", I continued to rant. "Why did I have to go off after those non-existent Lapland Buntings and Dotterel?"

"I dunno, Simon?" Chris continued smoothly. "I just can't think. I mean it was just so much easier strolling up here to the Garrison, and so much more successful. Anyway, let's go and get a drink. I need some nosh." He suggested making a move to leave for the Mermaid.

"Don't worry, Simon", Chris said soothingly as he supped his first pint. "They'll probably still be there tomorrow. I know it's spoilt your evening." He chuckled. "But RB Flickers and Barred Warblers are both pretty regular on Scilly." This just rubbed salt into the wound, and Chris knew it. For me, Red-breasted Flycatcher was a real bogey bird. The few times one had turned up in Christchurch I had missed them, usually because I had been away. Now I had missed two on Scilly. I could have stayed with the others so easily. People's bogey birds don't stay about. They may be common most years on Scilly, but I had a nasty feeling that Red-breasted Flycatchers were quite capable of giving the rest of 1984 a miss. With two excellent bird species on the Garrison, I knew exactly where I was going to be the next day.

5. *A quiet day on Scilly...almost*

This was a day during which I learned very little about birds...there were so few about. However, to my cost I did learn quite a lot about Scilly birding. I woke up early, full of enthusiasm and desperation to be out in the field. Having made everyone a cup of coffee, I was itching to get started.

Brian, Clive and I were out on the Garrison playing fields not long after. It was a glorious, dewy morning. The sun was just beginning to pierce the mist which lay in pockets over the island. The sky above was bright blue, and the air was still and becoming pleasantly warm. Unfortunately, though very pleasant for humans, this is not the sort of weather that blows birds off course to Scilly, much to the disappointment of Scilly birders. Rather, under these conditions, the birds tend to go where they were originally heading. We scanned the few birds feeding on the playing fields hoping for such treats as Tawny Pipits, Rose-coloured Starlings or even Lapland Buntings but saw none of them. However, we did see a beautifully marked Snow Bunting (known rather prosaically amongst Scilly birders as a snob!). It was a nice bird to see and a good start to the day.

Brian, having just started his holiday, had a date with the Blackpoll Warbler on St. Agnes. Clive had yet to see the Semi-p on Tresco, while Chris and Tessa were still in bed. Chris and Tessa had said they would catch up with me somewhere on St. Mary's when I had taken them their coffee. I wanted to see that Barred Warbler; I was also pretty desperate about those RB Flickers! I said goodbye to Brian and Clive, wishing them the best of luck, and set off as nonchalantly as I knew how to walk around the Garrison. Desperation in a birder does not go down well on Scilly and tends to make that birder a figure of fun. Soon I caught up with a group of people. They seemed to have found something which was at least encouraging.

"What are you on?" I asked casually as I wandered up to them.

"Two humming birds", they replied.

"Humming birds? You must be having me on." Then I caught sight of two Hummingbird Hawk Moths that were feeding on the nectar produced by some of the last flowers of the summer. They look like diminutive, brown hummingbirds as they hover from flower to flower. They were certainly good to see. After a while the group decided to walk on, so I joined them. We made our way slowly round to the Yellow-browed Warbler site.

"Any good?" we enquired casually of one of the half dozen or so birders standing there.

"One seen twenty minutes ago…flew over into those gardens, but not seen since." We stared at a rather attractive sunken garden for twenty minutes or so. No Yellow-browed Warblers! We strolled on and scanned bushes, gardens…the lot. We heard a strange bird call.

"What's that?" one of the group I was with muttered. The call came again. We stood in silence for a moment or two, scanning the trees and bushes nearby. None of us had a clue what it might be, though it did seem vaguely familiar. Next time the call appeared, binoculars shot up just in time to catch a giggling urchin diving off into the bushes. He was evidently well practiced at Scilly birder bating, a pastime which obviously gave him hours of fun, no doubt. A risky game that though. He could easily get himself lynched, especially when things were so quiet. We saw Holly Blue butterflies and other insects enjoying the warmth of the autumn sun, but exciting birds? … not a thing!

We proceeded slowly on. Suddenly a young lad with an uncharacteristic urgency came around the corner. It was the first urgency we had seen all day.

"Barred Warbler's showing well just around the corner", he announced. I felt an adrenal punch, and it took great self-control not to leave my newly found acquaintances and belt off after it. We moved slowly on and eventually caught up with a crowd of birders looking over a wall.

"Anyone on it?" I asked eagerly.

"Not recently", came the bored reply. "Last time it appeared it hopped up into that *Hebe* over there, but that was at least ten minutes ago." A *Hebe* is a bush rather like a cross between a Speedwell and a *Buddleia* and is common all over the islands. After just a minute or two, a plump little bird hopped up onto the *Hebe* and then flew across into a patch of bramble to feed on the berries.

On closer acquaintance, the bird seemed to grow in size, somehow. It was incredibly clumsy and made a considerable disturbance in the vegetation wherever it went. When it went any distance it shot off like a wayward bullet, landing with a complete lack of grace and causing a considerable commotion. This was a young, immature Barred Warbler, lacking the bars on the breast which give the species its name. I spent a happy half hour or so watching this enjoyable little comedy turn, then ambled on around the Garrison.

Still no sign of those RB Flickers...no sign of Chris and Tessa either. Slowly an uncomfortable awareness began to dawn that there were very few people about. Where was everyone? It was nearly lunchtime, so I walked down to the town to see if I could get any gen and find something to eat.

On my way I met one or two other birders who passed me

A long and patient vigil

aimlessly, or when asked if they knew of anything about replied casually, "Nothing special" and ambled on.

After a solitary pie and chips in the Mermaid, I thought I would go back up to the golf course and see if that Lapland Bunting had returned. On the way I spotted a Bar-tailed Godwit in a sandy bay. Then I very nearly put my foot in it by suggesting to two obviously experienced Scilly birders that a Rock Pipit I had just seen might actually be a Tawny Pipit. Well it did look rather big! Luckily for me, it failed to reappear.

I didn't actually get as far as the golf course, since the few birders who were walking in the other direction were so unenthusiastic about its present potential as a haven for Lapland Buntings that it didn't seem worth it. In any case, the afternoon was becoming pretty hot, and I was glad to have an excuse not to struggle up that hill again. Where was everyone!? Paranoia began to grip me. I could be missing out. The few birders I met were all in league persuading me that there was nothing about, while at the other end of the island everyone was enjoying a crippler!

Where were Chris and Tessa? I walked back towards the Garrison to have another go up there. It was now mid-afternoon and very warm indeed. A depressing lethargy began to set in as I struggled up the hill towards the playing fields. I began to walk around the Garrison once more and soon bumped into the group of birders who were still waiting in vain for the Yellow-browed Warblers. Neither had been seen now for several hours. I wandered on to a similar Barred Warbler group to hear that even that had given up. Perhaps they would have gen. They didn't. I lingered a little while and chatted. There was absolutely no news of anything else anywhere it seemed. This was ridiculous. Where was everyone!? I decided I would try and relax, enjoy the sun and spend a quiet hour or two under the group of pines where the RB Flickers had been seen. I wished I had had a book to read because there were no birds in those trees of any kind. After twenty minutes or so, a birder came around the corner and announced enigmatically, "There's a Streaky Warbler in Holy Vale!"

I had heard of neither Streaky Warbler nor Holy Vale but didn't want to show my ignorance. At least there was something positive to do. I headed off down the hill again in the direction of the town and asked the first person I met where Holy Vale was. He very kindly drew me a sketch map. By the time I found the place quite a number of birders were moving away muttering dismissively, "It's a Chiffchaff, only a Chiffchaff...a very slightly streaky Chiffchaff, and that's all it is."

Most of the birders in the whole of the Scilly Islands seemed to have been attracted to this place, yet there was no further news. I hadn't been missing out after all and felt a wave of relief. The idea of being gripped off yet again by Chris and Tessa would have been too much.

Having come all that way, I decided I might as well have a look at this Chiffchaff, just in case one of the real experts turned it into something more exotic later on. I wandered into Holy Vale. As its name implied, Holy Vale is an atmospheric, wooded valley with a stream and a raised path which threads itself between tree roots. It is very tranquil and ideal for birds. After a hundred yards or so I found a crowd of birders crammed into a small gap in a hedge. Beyond the gap was a clearing. Being tall, I could just see an osier bed beyond if I stood on tiptoe. Flitting around near the base of the osiers was a small, brown bird. It did look remarkably like a very ordinary Chiffchaff to me; it was indicative of how terribly quiet things were. Even a very ordinary Chiffchaff could become the bird of the moment. Everyone was so bored, they were trying desperately to see streaks all over it and turn it into something else. A flycatcher landed on a telegraph wire above the Chiffchaff crowd. It had absolutely no white on its tail and, unlike the warbler, had very obvious streaking on its breast. Reluctantly I decided that I couldn't turn it into a Red-breasted Flycatcher.

"There's a Peck Sand on Porth Hellick Pool", somebody announced. As there was absolutely nothing else to do, and Holy Vale was uncomfortably crowded, I decided I might as well go off and see this Pectoral Sandpiper. In any case, Porth Hellick Pool sounded interesting. If anyone had told me, even six weeks ago, that I would have been so nonchalant about an American wader I would not have believed him or her. Since this was to be my fourth Pectoral Sandpiper in as many weeks, it isn't that surprising that it failed to raise much enthusiasm in me.

Porth Hellick Pool is indeed a wonderful place for birds. I found the Pectoral Sandpiper quite easily and had some very pleasing views of a Water Rail sauntering along on the mud by the edge of the reeds. It had been a strange day and as I enjoyed some relaxed birding I felt content. I had also learnt something about Scilly – that even in this paradise for birds it is possible to have days when there is virtually nothing to see. It was the contrast with the excitement of the day before that had caused me to become paranoid. There was nothing else going to happen, so I decided to walk slowly back towards the town.

Suddenly a breathless messenger came running up the road full of news which he gasped as he caught up with people.

"Yellowthroat's been relocated on Bryher", he panted. "Boat's leaving in quarter of an hour from the quay." That's nice, I thought, but this is crazy. It's quarter to five and it'll be dark soon. However, since so many people were legging it as fast as they could towards the quay, I thought I'd better join them. I quickened my pace. I had walked a long way already that day and my feet were sore. All my leg muscles ached considerably. I came to a decision. If I arrived at the quay on time, I would take the boat to Bryher and try my luck. But I was damned if I was going to run for it though, as most other birders seemed to be doing. If I got there, I got there. If I didn't, there would always be tomorrow.

I arrived on the outskirts of the town to find the Jolly Green Giant sitting casually on a bench and looking out to sea.

"You're not rushing off to Bryher then", I observed as I joined him.

"No I am not", he replied positively. "It's not worth it; it's nearly dark. By the time that lot get there it really will be dark. The only ones getting anything out of this will be the boatmen."

I was grateful for the chance to rest my weary legs. A few late Sandwich Terns flew past lazily well out to sea.

"How did you get on, Brian?" I asked. "Did you catch up with the Blackpoll Warbler?"

"Yes I did", he replied enthusiastically. "What a little crippler! I saw it really well because I virtually had it to myself. Did you see those amazing canary-coloured feet?"

I had to admit to him that I hadn't.

"But they're it's best feature", he enthused. "Incredible colour. You know, you really ought to see those feet before you can say you've seen a Blackpoll Warbler properly. Anyway, I'm hungry! Let's go and find something to eat." We strolled towards the Mermaid, bumping into Chris and Tessa on the way. They seemed to have had an even quieter day than I had.

"You didn't go rushing off to Bryher then, Simon", Chris observed. "Looks as though Clive's the only one of our lot who has."

"He's wasting his time as well as his money", chuckled the Giant. "I can't wait to see his face when he gets back, all fed up and disappointed."

Brian, Chris, Tessa and I went to the Mermaid and enjoyed a really good slap-up meal. We sat at a window table, which overlooks the harbour, so we could see all the dejected forms and faces when the boats returned from Bryher. Sure enough, it was completely dark when the first boat arrived back. Then the second arrived, and there was even a third. There wasn't a happy face amongst them. Eventually Clive joined us in the Mermaid.

"Did you see it then?" Brian asked sarcastically, knowing full well what the answer would be.

"No, I bloody didn't! Of course I didn't!" he replied

petulantly. "Bloody waste of time."

"I could have told you that and saved you the bother", Brian teased. "Anyway, tell us all about it. What happened?"

"At four o'clock a Tresco boat was taking people off from Bryher", he began. "It had just left when this bloke was seen on the landing stage jumping up and down and waving his arms about like a windmill. I think most people thought he had simply missed the boat. Anyway he had a C.B., so he radioed St. Mary's and announced he'd just seen the Yellowthroat. When the Tresco boat got back to St. Mary's they all wanted to get back to Bryher as fast as possible."

"So when did you get there?" Brian asked.

"I was on one of the later boats", Clive continued. "A very few of the guys on the first boat did actually see it, but they only had the briefest glimpse. By the time our boat got there, everyone was thrashing about in the bracken and scaring the bird off completely. By then it was obvious it was not going to show: total bloody waste of time...and money!"

We finished our supper at a leisurely pace, it was delicious, and then went to join the others in the bar. There, sitting over their pints and looking incredibly smug, were two old friends of Chris and Tessa, called Leon and Bob. They were both very experienced birders and had life lists just short of the magic four hundred mark. They gave us the news that not only had the Yellowthroat been re-found on Bryher, but a Swainson's Thrush, which had put in the briefest appearance on St. Agnes a few days previously, had also been re-found. Leon and Bob had spent most of the day on St. Agnes looking for it. It hadn't been the happiest of experiences, they explained, because they had had to peer through little tunnels between apple trees all day. However, their efforts and suffering had been rewarded, because they had had glimpses of the Swainson's Thrush. Apart from the earlier sighting, they were still the only ones to have seen it. When arriving back on St. Mary's, they had been amongst the very first to hear of the Yellowthroat and had managed to get on that first boat going back to Bryher. As a result, they had been amongst the very few lucky ones to see the Yellowthroat. They were certainly the only ones on Scilly to have caught up with both birds.

"Two really ace cripplers in one day", they crowed. This was to be one of the very few occasions we were to see Leon happy. His moods were in direct proportion to the number of recent ticks he'd had. Having a long list, it was to be another ten days before he saw anything else he considered to be worthwhile.

In Britain, though I am told it is less the case in America, birding tends to be a thoroughly male pastime. British women just don't seem to be interested, and many marriages and promising relationships have foundered on the rocks as a result of birding. In the evening, conversation would often turn to female intolerance of a pursuit that most women considered a thorough waste of time. That evening, one of the birders told an amusing story about how he had dealt with his eavesdropping wife. He had a friend who was an airline pilot and a birder in his spare time.

"This is how I sorted her out", he began his story. "I rang up my airline pilot friend and said, 'How about this Aleutian Tern in Greenland?' I knew she'd be listening to our conversation on the extension in the bedroom. 'Could you get hold of a Jumbo Jet for a day or two?' I continued. 'At £200 per head, we could fill it easily.'

'That shouldn't be a problem,' the pilot replied who was in on the hoax. 'We'd better make sure we've got everything we need. We'll need flasks of coffee...and how about some prawn sandwiches. At £200 a head they'll need a little luxury. When do you reckon we should go?'" At the time it was mid-March.

'How about the beginning of April', was the reply.

'Sounds fine', replied the pilot. 'I'll get on with it and make the arrangements. You get your wife to make those prawn sandwiches.' He put the phone down, and I just waited long enough to hear the click on the extension as she put her phone down too. You should have seen her doing those sandwiches! Anyway, the night we were due to leave came round. I put on the alarm and went to bed. At three o'clock it went off. She shook me and said, 'Come on, time to get up and go off to Greenland.' I woke up just long enough to say, 'April Fool!' then rolled over and went back to sleep again. I had never actually told her I was going. She just assumed it from listening to my telephone calls. I must admit I did have a bit of a chuckle when she asked when I wanted those prawn sandwiches!"

In the evening, talk was always about birds of one sort or another, though quite a few birders were pretty keen on butterflies as well. There was always at least one other woman in the Mermaid and that was the pretty barmaid who served us. A few days later, a birder I knew persuaded her to go with him to try and see the Yellowthroat. I bumped into them just as they were arriving at the site where the Yellowthroat had last been seen. After one minute she demanded, "Where's this Yellowthroat then?" After three she continued with, "This is boring. Do you mean to tell me you blokes just stand about all day staring at these bushes? You must be completely out of your minds…and just for some stupid little bird."

He never did see the Yellowthroat because they left after she had been waiting for it for just five minutes. Over the next day or two, we were to find out that Yellowthroat watching is only for the most dedicated birders. In no way can it be recommended as entertainment for potential girlfriends. That short-lived relationship ended on the return boat to St. Mary's.

6. *The Yellowthroat...and how we suffered for it!*

To my astonishment next morning none of us seemed particularly keen to do anything. Deep down we all knew that this Yellowthroat was going to require a great deal of patience and suffering before we saw it, and we felt about as keen on embarking on it as having a swim on a grey, wet afternoon in the North Sea! Two early boats had been laid on for the keenest birders. At seven thirty, a boat had left for the Yellowthroat on Bryher, while another had left with birders anxious to see the Swainson's Thrush on St. Agnes. We heard later that most people on that early boat to Bryher did see the Yellowthroat. Having got up that early, I reckoned they had deserved their success. Those on the St. Agnes boat had brief glimpses of the Swainson's Thrush as well.

The first thing I did that morning was to go with the Giant to buy provisions in the town. We left the supermarket with an enormous box full of stuff which was very heavy. We agreed to take it in turns to carry it up to Greystones. I managed to stagger with it for a few yards when the Giant, making light of it, effortlessly lifted it onto his shoulders and carried it all the way. By the time we got back, a heavy and penetrating mist had begun to smother the islands which was most unpleasant. The others were up, breakfasted and ready for a day's birding when we arrived with the groceries. We took a slow and damp walk around the Garrison but hardly saw a thing. Visibility was down to a few yards, and only birds that we took by surprise could be seen at all as they dashed off into the gloom. There was no sign of Barred Warbler, Yellow-browed Warbler or the

Snow Bunting. There was certainly no evidence of any Red-breasted Flycatchers. The others managed a Blackcap and a Garden Warbler, but I missed them both. My bird of the morning was a Lesser Black-backed Gull.

At lunchtime we went down to the Porthcressa to see if there was any news. The early morning sightings of the Yellowthroat and Swainson's Thrush were on the board, but there was nothing else new. Radio Birdbrain in its corner was utterly quiet. We had a pasty and a hot drink and then decided on a course of action. I was pretty certain that under the prevailing conditions no one was going to see the Yellowthroat and, with his experience of the previous evening, Clive had had more than enough of it for the time being. Initially Clive and I thought we might try for the Swainson's Thrush on St. Agnes, while the others went off to Bryher for the Yellowthroat. We were just finalising arrangements when Leon came in and asked us what we were going to do.

"You might just see the Yellowthroat if you're extremely lucky", he offered his depressing opinion. "But the Swainson's...not a chance! It is such a skulker that in this weather at any rate you just wouldn't see it." Outside, the drizzle was becoming appreciably heavier. The idea of peering down little tunnels beneath small trees in a dripping apple orchard to see a bird that wouldn't appear in any case did not appeal in the least. I tossed a coin.

"Head's Yellowthroat, tails Swainson's". The coin spun through the air. I was relieved when the coin showed heads. "Right, I've changed my mind", I announced decisively. "I'm off to Bryher for the Yellowthroat." Clive remained adamant after his experiences with the Yellowthroat, he was still going to St. Agnes.

As our boat swung from the quay and left for Bryher, we

Looking out towards Tresco and Bryher from St. Mary's

could see the forlorn figure of Clive with one or two other birders waiting to leave for St. Agnes. When we arrived on Bryher, the drizzle was, if anything, even more penetrating. We walked along a pebble-strewn beach, crushing Kaffir Fig beneath our boot-clad feet. Kaffir Fig is a plant that has been introduced into much of southern Britain from South Africa. Its leaves look very like green potato chips. This plant is everywhere on the beaches of Bryher. I tasted a leaf once because its Latin name is *Carpobrotus edulis*. Any plant with '*edulis*' in its name is generally edible. Actually, it was quite revolting and very bitter.

As we approached a large and depressingly wet crowd of birders, we came across the couple I had met looking at the Hummingbird Hawk Moths. They were just leaving.

"Any luck?" I asked.

"We had ever such a brief glimpse of it about ten minutes ago", they replied. "But that was the first sighting since seven o'clock this morning." We thanked them and went to join the crowd. At that rate it seemed to be putting in a brief appearance every six hours! What chance did we have? Pretty slim, I reckoned. As we joined the crowd, we were confronted by a featureless hillside covered with bracken and gorse bushes. The gorse bushes were festooned with delicate spiders' webs suspending jewel-like droplets of water. We asked our fellow birders where the bird was supposed to be, and the general opinion seemed to be that it was lurking in the bottom of a rather distressed and isolated apple tree which grew opposite us on the other side of a dry stone wall. A large number of sodden telescopes were aiming at the bottom of that tree, though few were being looked through at that moment. Apathy was creeping into those who had been there any length of time, and it wouldn't be long before it was affecting us all. In any case, it wasn't certain whether or not the bird was in the apple tree any more. The last time it had been seen, evidently, it was in the gorse.

We began our damp and depressing vigil. Occasionally, the lightest breeze would move a leaf causing a minor stir amongst the crowd. A Stonechat would stand cockily on the upper most twigs of the apple tree, or a Robin would sing plaintively from its deeper recesses. One lucky chap's boredom was relieved when a Scilly or Lesser White-toothed Shrew, *Crocidura suaveolens*, scrambled over the top of his boot. From those who had been lucky enough to glimpse the bird earlier, we heard that it had a throat and upper breast of incredibly intense canary yellow. As it was, our distressed apple tree was full of pendulous and very ripe canary yellow Golden Delicious.

Innumerable bored birders had amused themselves by estimating the number of apples in that tree. The consensus seemed to be that there were about sixty, and when any one of them moved slightly it could persuade the more optimistic of us that it was a Yellowthroat.

As the afternoon wore on, so the weather became more and more depressingly wet, and the light began to fade. As the weather became wetter, so did we. Water found its way beneath collars and ran uncomfortably down the comparative warmth of backs. We were standing on an upper beach consisting of large, unstable pebbles. Every time we moved our feet, shuffling in a vain attempt to keep warm, we were in dire danger of losing our balance. This in turn would make a noise that could disturb the bird in the extremely unlikely event of it still being there. Noises of this sort would cause neighbouring birders to whisper "Ssssh!" urgently. The whole experience was quite, quite awful. This was real suffering, yet we were all supposed to be on holiday.

An aged islander with an air of total unconcern sauntered past on the other side of the wall, between the crowd of birders and the apple tree, making our silent vigil all a bit pointless. In spite of an audience of some five hundred silent Barbour-clad witnesses, he didn't bat an eyelid. There was an official pathway in front of us, so he was completely within his rights. I must say that, if I had had such a grimly determined audience watching me, I would have felt some embarrassment, to say the least.

Apart from the very occasional activity at the bottom of the apple tree, which always turned out to be a Wren, a Robin or a Goldcrest, but never a Yellowthroat, the only excitement occurred when we heard the unmistakable sound of boots running over pebbles. That sound is always a sure sign that something is happening. I joined the rush only to find that, like most of the others, I had arrived just too late to see the Rough-legged Buzzard which had just sailed past overhead. After this minor excitement, there was nothing for it but to go and continue staring at those damned Golden Delicious. Even if we had wanted to head back for St. Mary's, there wasn't another boat for hours.

The face of Lee Evans, a well-known birding fanatic, suddenly materialized a foot behind the apple tree. This gave us all quite a shock at first, but he was being quite a hero in fact because, had the bird been in that tree, he might well have gently coaxed it out into full view for the rest of us, whilst if the bird were to appear, he would almost certainly be the only one who would not see it. However, it was soon blatantly obvious that even if the Yellowthroat had been in that tree earlier, it certainly wasn't there any more. People began to shuffle, talk and joke in their misery, and the inevitable conclusion that we should give it up as a bad job began to take hold.

Feeling damp and depressed, a column of misery began to shuffle back towards the quay and the four thirty boat back to St. Mary's. On arriving back in St. Mary's, the first thing we did was to go round to the Porthcressa to find out that there was nothing new except the vague report of a Dotterel up on the airport. Since it was still over an hour until opening time, and there really was nothing else to do, we trudged up there. By the time we had got to the airport, if anything, it was drizzling even harder than ever. It had become even more misty, and this made visibility very poor indeed. In the great expanse of grass in front of us, we could just about make out the ghostly outline of birds in the gloom. Most of the birds flew off long before we got within identification range; those that didn't turned out invariably to be Meadow Pipits or Lapwing. The best thing I found was a field mushroom; it went very well next morning with my eggs and bacon, much to the consternation of the others who were convinced it was some poisonous sort.

Feeling very bedraggled, we returned to the Mermaid. It was six o'clock and on the stroke of opening time. We had to make a stop at the pub in any case, as Chris and Tessa had left our groceries in there, which included our supper.

"We'll just have a quick one", said Chris conspiratorially. We were still in there several hours later at closing time reviving our flagging spirits. It wasn't long before Clive joined us. He was equally bedraggled; if anything, he had had an even worse experience than us on St. Agnes, if that were possible. Needless to say, he hadn't seen the Swainson's Thrush.

"How were things on St. Agnes, then?" Brian asked.

"Awful", Clive groaned as he made short work of the first half of the pint of beer in front of him. "Drizzle all the time, the trees overhead dripping rain down our necks, and all the time having to concentrate on those tiny gaps between the trees. I never want to see that ruddy parsonage again. It was in the grounds of the St. Agnes Parsonage that the orchard with the Swainson's Thrush was situated. How about you? Did you get your Yellowthroat?" We resisted the temptation to grip him off, which under the circumstances would have been both unethical and grossly unfair.

"Did we hell!" Chris exclaimed. "Join the club. It was awful, truly appalling", and Chris outlined for Clive's benefit the rigours of the afternoon. The evening wore on. By eight o'clock I was starving and went up to the restaurant for a meal; somehow the others made do with a simple diet of beer all evening.

Just before closing time, news filtered through from the Log at the Porthcressa that a Solitary Sandpiper had been seen on Porth Hellick Pool. The Solitary Sandpiper is one of the rarer

North American waders that visit Britain from time to time and constituted another challenge.

"Damn and Blast!!" I expostulated. I had just got used to the idea of spending from now until eternity on the Yellowthroat when this Solitary Sandpiper had to come along and complicate matters.

"Why the hell couldn't it have been more considerate and waited until we'd got the Yellowthroat safely UTB", I demanded.

"One tick at a time, that's all I ask, Sweet Jesus, one tick at a time", Brian sang quietly to himself in the background, beaming all over his face. He was alright, he had already seen a Solitary Sandpiper before, and so had all the others, as I soon found out.

At eleven o'clock we left the Mermaid. As we strolled back drunkenly to Greystones we realised that since only those on the early boat had seen the Yellowthroat, we would have to get up early and catch that seven thirty boat. As we wandered back, it all seemed so simple – we would have to get up at six o'clock. What is that they say about hell… and roads being paved with good intentions?

We were pretty inebriated. We staggered out of the pub and tried to teeter up a wall next to the steps leading up to the Garrison. With much swaying and near loss of balance, both Chris and the Jolly Green Giant managed it. In years to come and on subsequent visits to Scilly, we were all to manage it both forwards and backwards, and from the top downwards. On this occasion, I managed a few feet only before toppling off.

By now the mist had turned into a dense pea-soup fog. At regular intervals, an eerie upturned hoot reached us out of the gloom across the sea. It sounded rather like a sea cow must sound mourning its dead; this was the Tresco lighthouse. After a few seconds, St. Agnes would reply with a deep, throaty "Boooooooooop!" When we arrived back at Greystones, we made a vain attempt to sober up with black coffee, set alarm clocks and then rolled into bed.

7. A much better day...after a bad start

The day started both prematurely and badly for me at four o'clock in the morning. I woke with a mouth feeling like the bottom of a parrot cage. I looked at my watch and realised the time, poured myself a glass of water and went back to bed and tried to get back to sleep again. The next time I awoke it was with a start. I looked at my watch. It said eight o'clock. The air went a violent shade of blue. I went into the other room where Clive and Brian were sleeping peacefully. Both had alarm clocks and had promised to wake the rest of us up.

"What the hell's going on?" I raved. "Do you know what time it is?" I suppose I was particularly put out because I had slept badly. A dull groan issued from the general direction of the Jolly Green Giant.

"Do you want coffee?" I asked grumpily. "You don't deserve it. I'm going off down to Porth Hellick to see the Solitary Sandpiper. I'll see you both on the ten fifteen boat to Bryher; that's if you manage to get up in time!" I added sarcastically. I made coffee for everyone and took a cup through to Chris and Tessa.

"They both overslept", I informed them angrily. "So we've missed the early boat."

"Oh well", Chris muttered sleepily, "Never mind", rolled over and went back to sleep. It says something for the way this Scilly birding business can grab you that I was so upset. Normally, I'm sure I wouldn't have got so worked up about it. To me it was a matter of life and death now that I see this Yellowthroat.

It was half past eight when I left Greystones. The weather was now quite pleasant, although still overcast. I had an hour and three quarters before the next boat would leave for Bryher. I walked quite fast in the general direction of Porth Hellick via the airport, just in case a Dotterel had decided to put in an appearance. Several birders were up there when I arrived. A Dotterel had been spotted, but the airport had had a noisy fire drill, and everything had flown off.

I took a scenic, coastal route from the airport down to Porth Hellick. The air was fresh, and the exercise was doing me good: clearing my brain after the excesses of the previous evening. By the time I reached Porth Hellick, I was feeling good. By the time I reached the Porth Hellick hide, the morning had become quite warm, and I felt hot as I was wearing the usual birder's uniform of jacket, heavy pullover and boots.

The hide was packed, and there was a queue of people outside waiting to get in. Some birders were looking through a gap in the fence to the right of the path leading to the hide. I joined them. In front of us on the mud opposite, close to the edge of a reed bed, strutted a dark-backed wader. It looked like a Green Sandpiper. It was really very close, close enough to see a prominent eye ring, a feature of Solitary Sandpipers. I didn't see it fly though, so was unable to confirm that it lacked a white rump. From the views I had of the bird walking over the mud, there was no suspicion of one. I was convinced that the bird I was looking at was indeed the Solitary Sandpiper and so was a bit surprised that none of the waiting birders were taking much notice of it. Perhaps they wanted to see it in the comfort of the hide, or, alternatively, their identification abilities were not so good, and they needed to have the bird pointed out to them. The Solitary Sandpiper strutted off to the left and disappeared from my view. A Water Rail wandered out onto the mud only five yards away.

I looked at my watch. It was nine thirty and if I didn't want to miss another boat to Bryher, I needed to start back. I had just enough time to buy myself a pasty and a can of orangeade. I was starving. In my haste to see the Solitary Sandpiper, I hadn't had time for any breakfast at Greystones. I sauntered down to the quay devouring my pasty and bought a ticket for the boat. The others were already there waiting on the quay. I looked around for a waste bin to lose my orangeade can in. As there was none to be seen, I stuffed the can deep into my pocket and went to join the others.

The route the boat took to Bryher was longer than usual. Because of the state of the tide, we had to land on another part of the island. As we passed Samson we saw the head of an Atlantic Grey Seal swimming towards the shore. It hauled itself up onto a seaweed-covered rock. Samson is one of the smaller, uninhabited islands. Every rock close to the island was densely crowded with Shags, and a few Gannet and Kittiwake glided past us effortlessly. The air and sea were calm, and there was just the slightest ocean swell which gently disturbed the seaweed on the shore as we went by. I found out later that, as we passed Samson, one or two on our boat had seen the Rough-legged Buzzard sitting on a rock, but I didn't. For a little while we ploughed our way through waters which were scarcely shielded by reefs from the open Atlantic. In spite of the calm, we could see huge waves breaking over the outermost rocks of the islands. Further out great sheets of water and foam were being hurled into the air, and, as the wave sucked away from the rocks, rivulets of foam ran like streams of volcanic lava off the smooth, black rocks. Although the sea surface was still smooth, the increased swell caused our boat to buck about a bit. Eventually we arrived at the point we were to make our landing on Bryher.

Our landing was to be on a beach with boulders covered in seaweed, which was brown, very wet and slippery. I had noticed that most of the boats carried a plank of wood tied to the prow of the boat; we were about to find out what those planks were for. To make the shore, we had to leave the boat by the prow and walk to the shore along a plank which was no more than nine inches wide. The first six feet or so of this short journey were over gently undulating, but very deep, sea. Huge fronds of brown kelp waved sinuously many fathoms beneath the surface. Once we had safely gained the shore, we slipped and slithered over the seaweed-covered rocks; the chances of remaining upright seemed slim.

"Boats will leave at 2.45pm and at 4.30pm from the quay", the boatman announced as each of us left the boat. We walked along the shore from the opposite direction to the previous day, but all too soon there was that wretched apple tree with a huge phalanx of birders in front of it waiting patiently for the Yellowthroat to appear. We asked anxiously whether it had been seen at all and were told that, as yesterday, it had put in a brief appearance soon after the early boat had arrived but had not been seen since. After the usual greetings and pleasantries, which occur when a new boatload of birders join a vigil, we settled down to wait. Seconds turned into minutes, and, unbelievably, minutes turned into hours. The passage of time seemed to have been suspended. I noticed that I still had the empty orangeade can in my pocket and it got in the way when I wanted to warm my hands. Although I was sorely tempted, my conscience wouldn't let me lose it into the *Pittosporum*. It says something for the aching boredom of that vigil that problems of an awkward orangeade can remain such a vivid memory.

Our boredom was relieved a little by a birder with a north-country accent and a lively sense of humour. He said he was simply dying for a cup of tea but knew that if he left, just for five minutes, the Yellowthroat would be bound to appear. We amused ourselves by talking about the absurd directions birders sometimes give when trying to indicate the whereabouts of a bird. Once when I was sea watching, a birder had described the position of a bird as, "just above the large wave halfway to the horizon!" The hillside in front of us was as featureless as the sea. Waves were replaced by gorse bushes and tufts of bracken with very few features which characterised them. There was the occasional seedling pine, and we would just have to hope that if the Yellowthroat did appear it would choose to hop up onto one of those. Inevitably during the morning, a small brown bird, probably a Chiffchaff, had caused a momentary stir by offering itself as a Yellowthroat candidate.

"It's just above the pale leaf in the mushroom-shaped gorse bush", said the birder who'd found it, enigmatically; there were a remarkable number of mushroom-shaped gorse bushes on that hillside. Time dragged on. Occasionally to relieve boredom, we scanned the shore for waders. At least it was something to do. There were Turnstones, Oystercatchers and Ringed Plovers in good numbers. A small number of birders tried to string something out of a Grey Plover without success, that is except to kill another ten minutes. The vigil went on, and on...and on. It was very tedious. For something to do, I announced to the birder next to me, "The Yellowthroat will appear in exactly one minute...I predict it!" Of course it didn't, and my skills as a clairvoyant were reckoned pretty suspect when after a full hour the Yellowthroat still hadn't appeared. At lunchtime, one or two birders, and especially those who had arrived on the earlier boat, began to feel very hungry and moved away to search for a café reputed to be amongst the houses away in the distance. To make matters worse, after we had been standing for two hours, it started to drizzle again.

Scarcely anyone noticed when a birder whispered urgently, "I've got it...it's on top of the wall...there's a spiky bush about six foot from...damn! It's dropped." I had managed to find the spot he was talking about just in time to see a little brown bird dive into the undergrowth. Presumably it had been the Yellowthroat, but from what I had seen I couldn't have distinguished it from the back view of a Wren, a Robin or even a Chiffchaff! The next few moments were extremely tense and all but unbearable, not only for me but, I am sure, for everyone else who had had inadequate views. However, there seemed little doubt that that little flash of brown had been the Yellowthroat. Could I say I'd seen it? More important, could I tick it? I was just coming to the conclusion that I couldn't, at least I hope that was the conclusion I was coming to, when the bird hopped up onto a piece of bramble close to the spot where it had disappeared.

"There it is!... it's back again... it's hopped back up onto the wall... WHAT A CRIPPLER!!!... that yellow on the throat, it's INCREDIBLE!!... you can actually see traces of a mask... that means it's a male coming into full plumage...what an utterly amazing little darling... it's still there, this is just incredible... Oh wow!!!... What an absolutely stonking little bird," etc., etc., etc. Very few birds are sufficiently crippling to be described as stonking, which might actually be the ultimate accolade. It was generally agreed, however, that this Yellowthroat was a real stonker!

This Yellowthroat behaved rather like a *Phylloscopus* warbler, which is the group of small grey species such as Chiffchaff, Willow Warbler and even Yellow-browed Warbler. I have now had several experiences of a number of yellowthroat species on the other side of the Atlantic. Without exception, they are all skulking and rarely offer prolonged views of themselves. However, this particular Yellowthroat was bobbing and weaving its way along the base of the wall in front of us. Far from being skulking, it was actually giving a very prolonged performance. Much to the delight of its considerable audience, it would turn to present its throat to us, giving vivid flashes of yellow. This extracted further "Wows" and "Aaaahs" from its avid admirers. Having invested a lot of time, patience and discomfort on this bird, everyone was feeling in a state of considerable euphoria. Very slowly a wave of decorous applause spread along the line of birders, hand clapping of the sort one might expect to give visiting royalty.

"Not yet", whispered Tessa urgently. "It's still there! Wouldn't it be better to wait till it's gone?" She needn't have worried, because apart from giving a bob or two to its fans the Yellowthroat didn't seem to take a great deal of notice. Obviously it didn't know it was the cause of the applause, but who knows, it may have sensed the appreciation and well-being it had created amongst us. It would be nice to think so, anyway.

All the time the Yellowthroat was working its way steadily towards our right in the general direction of a group of *Fuchsia* bushes, which were covered in vivid, flame coloured blossom. A birder returning from the café heard the applause and broke into a run. This turned into the fastest sprint his boot-clad feet would allow. He arrived and asked breathlessly.

"Is it showing?"

"Yes, it's just below the *Fuchsia*, above that rather sharp stone in the wall. It's been moving to the right for some time now."

"I've got you", he said, but before he actually got onto the bird the Yellowthroat had dived back into the undergrowth.

"There's some poor bloke here still hasn't seen it", someone shouted in a loud voice. "Anyone still on it?" A wave of sympathy for the guy went through the crowd; it was almost tangible. It didn't do any good, though. For the time being at least, the Yellowthroat had taken its curtain call. However, it did show again that day at around four o'clock. For the chap who had arrived on the scene just too late, that must have been a pretty grim hour or two.

When the euphoria had subsided sufficiently for us to consider what we might do next, it was just two o'clock. We had nearly three quarters of an hour before the next boat back to St. Mary's. We suddenly realised just how hungry we were and decided to go off in search of the café which was rumoured to exist. When eventually we tracked it down it turned out to be a rather small, hut-like affair with a corrugated iron roof. It was doing a roaring trade in toast, coffee and tea. Not generally being renowned as one of the best birding islands, I don't think Bryher had had such an invasion before and wasn't really geared up for it. Even at the height of the summer season, it is not one of the most visited islands. As well as sustenance, I found a dustbin into which I gratefully jettisoned my orangeade can.

Even though the boat back to St. Mary's brimmed over with euphoria, these feelings were not matched by the weather which was deteriorating again. Once more the descended mist was turning into a fine and penetrating drizzle. By the time the boat arrived at the quay, everyone was thoroughly wet through. When we got back we went round to the Porthcressa to see what was on the board. Boldly written across the top was:

Yellowthroat   *Bryher Showing well 2pm*

It felt really great to know that we had been there at the right time to witness it happening. There were other interesting entries on the board:

Lapland Bunting   *Old Town Road*
Common Rosefinch   *Porth Hellick*

As I hadn't managed to catch up with Lapland Buntings either on the golf course or the airport, these were two more potential ticks. Even though the weather was now pretty foul and the light dingy to say the least, we trudged off in the direction of Old Town Road, leading from Hugh Town to Porth Hellick, to see what we could see. Incredibly, I had already visited Porth Hellick that morning to see the Solitary Sandpiper; it seemed a very long time ago.

As we walked out of Hugh Town we could easily tell where the Lapland Bunting was. A group of about a dozen birders were leaning on a gate and staring into a field. We joined them. Beyond the gate was a ploughed field with deep ruts carved across it. The ruts were at least a foot deep. Fields like this are a feature of Scilly in the autumn and don't make birding any easier. More often than not, the birds are skulking around in the bottom of the ruts. Matters are made worse by the dying remnants of tall weeds, such as dock and fat hen. In many cases, the ripe seed shed by the weeds is the reason the birds are there in the first place. At least the weeds can have their uses for the birders as they often have bizarre shapes and can be used as pointers.

About ten yards from the gate a flock of sparrows was feeding busily, occasionally making itself visible as it moved over ruts and between vegetation. My friends tried to indicate to me which of these sparrows was in fact a Lapland Bunting. I tried really hard, convinced I was studying the bird beneath the right chicken-shaped dock, but could see nothing except for House Sparrows. In the end a kind fellow birder let me look through his scope, which he had trained onto it, and I saw immediately that it was a fairly distinctive little bird. Although these little finches, sparrows and buntings may look distinctive enough in the books where they are invariably depicted as breeding males in full summer plumage, when seen in Scilly in the autumn, however, more often than not they are juveniles. If they are not actually the current year's nestlings, they will either be females or winter plumage males. To make matters worse, they will be hopping about frenetically amongst pieces of vegetation or skulking down in ruts in company with literally hundreds of other birds that look almost identical to them. A quick glance at any field guide will show that most female buntings, even the rarest, look remarkably like female sparrows outside the breeding season.

After I had managed to have a good look at the Lapland Bunting, we walked on to Porth Hellick. By the time we got there, the light was getting worse by the minute, and the drizzle heavier and even more penetrating. As I was still the only one to have seen this particular Solitary Sandpiper, the others went off to the shelter of the main hide. I wandered off to the other end of the pool where there was a group hoping to catch a glimpse of the Common Rosefinch. Common Rosefinches used to be called Scarlet Grosbeaks in the older guide books, and, as always, the male is illustrated in its breeding plumage. In full breeding plumage it is an attractive species with a bright red bib and a generous beak. In autumn, when they visit the Scilly Isles, they are more or less uniform grey with little in the way of distinguishing features except a feint wing bar.

"Has it been seen?" I asked as I joined the group.

"About ten minutes ago in that hawthorn over there", came

the reply from a helpful birder. "Trouble is, it flew down that line of trees to the left. It does that from time to time, but it'll probably be back. You had better hurry though, because this light's getting diabolical."

"What's the recent news on the Solitary Sand?" I asked.

"Oh that's gone", they replied. "Hasn't been seen since mid-afternoon." It slowly dawned on me then that things had really turned out rather well, for me at least. Had we managed to get up in time for the seven o'clock boat we would only have had grotty, early morning views of the Yellowthroat. We would almost certainly have been very bored indeed by two o'clock and would probably have either been in the café or on the way back to St. Mary's and have missed the really good views. One thing is certain, I would not have seen the Solitary Sandpiper. I suddenly felt immensely grateful to Brian and Clive for oversleeping and made a mental note to buy them a drink. It is strange how sometimes things can work out so well.

The scene around me at Porth Hellick had a strange, unearthly quality about it. Telescopes were draped with sheets of polythene in a vain attempt to keep out the water. The tripods, binoculars, birders' noses, everything had droplets of water suspended from them; there was water everywhere. I looked through my binoculars and was rewarded with indistinct shapes in a dull grey mist. It occurred to me that I would spot any birds that might come along better without the bins. I did have a rain-guard which should help to keep the eyepieces moisture free, but the lenses were smeared with condensation, and it was impossible to keep them dry. The tissues I had taken with me that morning, especially for that purpose, were now an unpleasant, shapeless soggy mass in the bottom of my pocket. I tried using my shirttail with only partial success.

There was a slight stir down the line of bedraggled birders;

the chap nearest to me said he could see the bird. I tried as hard as I could, yet could see nothing but a grey mist through my binoculars. A chap with a telescope let me have a quick look at the bird, as it was a lifer for me. I just caught sight of a grey blob, which was indistinguishable from any other grey species of bird, when it dropped into the undergrowth. To me the blob didn't seem to have a particularly large beak, and the wing bars were totally impossible to see. I had to reckon that I had had three and perhaps a half lifer ticks during the day, and that's pretty good by any standards.

We had all decided to give up when a pathetic little warbler poked its head up in the reeds in front of us. It was so incredibly wet that all its head feathers were clinging to its skull. It looked like one of those wretched popeyed creatures one sometimes sees in inferior museum displays. It was an *Acrocephalus* warbler (Reed and Sedge Warbler group) and in its present condition was indistinguishable from a Reed Warbler. Someone had reported a Marsh Warbler earlier; almost certainly wishful thinking as they can only be distinguished with any degree of certainty on their song. I suppose that poor, bedraggled creature in front of us was the stringy Marsh Warbler. Even though potentially another lifer, I couldn't possibly turn it into yet another tick for the day.

Feeling rather like the Reed/Marsh Warbler, I squelched my way back to the Garrison and a much-needed hot bath. That evening Tessa made us all supper. It was a really excellent chilli con carne, which revitalised our spirits considerably. Most of the earlier Yellowthroat euphoria had returned by the time we went down to the Mermaid to celebrate. As we were in a celebratory mood we bought a bottle of wine to have back at Greystones after the pub had closed.

"I've got Yellowthroat on my list", crowed a smiling Jolly Green Giant. "And no bugger can ever take it off it!"

8. *The Swainson's Thrush...and the Great Grip Off!!*

Next morning the position on the Isles of Scilly, apart from those birds we had already seen and according to the board at the Porthcressa, was as follows:

Red-breasted Flycatcher	*Trenoweth, St. Mary's*
Swainson's Thrush	*St. Agnes*
? American Cuckoo species	*Bryher*

I had been assured by everyone that Red-breasted Flycatchers were usually a regular occurrence on Scilly in the autumn, but that the chances of re-finding the one at Trenoweth were very slim. We had heard the vague rumour of an American cuckoo flying over a pool on Bryher, and it was more than likely that this bird, whatever it was, had left the Isles of Scilly completely. That left the Swainson's Thrush.

"I'm off to see the Swainson's Thrush", I announced as we made plans over breakfast. The Giant had set his heart on going to St. Martin's where he was convinced he was going to turn up the Crippler of 1984. He was convinced that St. Martin's, an island rarely visited by birders, was under-watched, and that all kinds of amazing rarities were being missed as a result. He had been looking at the *Field Guide to the Birds of North America* and had set his heart on finding a Worm-eating Warbler to get his name into the ornithological history books. Worm-eating Warblers are even pretty rare in the States where they come from. He was going around the bungalow psyching himself up by singing catch phrases such as "One tick at a time, that's all I ask, Sweet Jesus, one tick at a time." He sang this to the tune of a pop song which was popular at the time. If it wasn't this he would be shouting, "Come on, you cripplers!" as a football fan might shout. "We are the champions!" Chris and Tessa were still fast asleep, so that just left Clive. He decided he would stay on St. Mary's and see what he could turn up for himself.

As I left for the quay and the boat for St. Agnes, it was a brilliant, warm and sunny day. What a wonderful contrast it was to the weather of yesterday and the day before. On my way down to the quay I noticed that the view through my binoculars wasn't very clear. I looked through them in reverse and, to my horror, could see a small disc of grey condensation on the inside of the large lens. By the time I arrived at the quay, the disc had grown and completely covered the whole of both lenses. Looking through them, my view was reduced to a milky haze. This was infuriating. In my opinion my binoculars were far from cheap, and they had let me down at this crucial moment when I was off to see a rare American visitor. Someone with similar binoculars explained that the barrels of the binoculars could be unscrewed and, by pointing them at the sun, the condensation should evaporate, particularly on a warm, sunny day like the one we had. In fact, compared with the price of top-of-the-range binoculars that shouldn't let in water in this way, my binoculars were really very cheap. But at that time, I did not know this. Much later I discovered that unscrewing binoculars is an unwise thing to do. The inside of binoculars is treated with a very carefully applied film of grease. Once disturbed, this becomes smeared, and the binoculars are costly to repair as a result. By unscrewing the barrels, the binoculars also become less watertight. In spite of taking this drastic action, I could still see that there was condensation on the prisms deep inside the binoculars. I felt a wave of desperate frustration pass through me. They were still virtually useless, and there seemed to be nothing I could do about it, especially as I was sitting on a boat about to leave for St. Agnes.

The boat was about to depart when someone woke me from my deliberations by calling my name. There on the quay stood the Jolly Green Giant.

"I thought you were off to Martin's", I observed. He was far from amused.

"I was the only one who wanted to go", he grumbled. "They wouldn't put a boat on just for me, so I'll have to come to St. Agnes with you after all." He was very fed up.

As we sped across to St. Agnes, my mood improved by the minute because my binoculars improved rapidly. The Giant explained that he had had the same problem with his telescope. In many ways, his telescope was his trademark. I have already stated that he was a pretty big bloke. His telescope was correspondingly small, just about a foot long. The telescope was attached to a monopod just over six feet tall. The whole thing looked rather like an out of proportion polo stick and he was never without it.

Once we had disembarked, we proceeded towards the post office once more. A small group of birders were watching a Melodious Warbler, so we joined them. It was a charming little grey bird with a bright yellow throat and a colourful beak, diving in and out of a dense *Pittosporum* hedge looking for food. Melodious Warblers often have a yellow patch beneath the beak in the autumn, but this one was almost rivalling the Yellowthroat in terms of brilliance.

"It's stained with caterpillar juice!" exclaimed the Giant.

We walked on towards the Parsonage and the Swainson's Thrush. Every crack and gap in the wall which surrounded the Parsonage had an expectant birder crouched against it. At the entrance to the Parsonage itself was a queue of people, birders waiting in turn to go into the garden and try for a glimpse of the bird of the moment. Arrangements had been made with the owners to allow about thirty people in at a time. One or two of the old-hand Scilly birders had taken it upon themselves to organise things for us. The bird hadn't put in an appearance since seven thirty that morning, so there was a very long queue. Brian and I decided that, for the moment at least, attempting to see the Swainson's Thrush was a fool's errand. As a result, we spent the rest of the morning wandering around the island. "Doing some proper birding", as Brian put it. It was a glorious morning with the sun shining strongly. We saw prodigious numbers of common migrants, and there were lots of butterflies flitting about. It was hard to believe that it really was October.

A fat, and self-satisfied tabby cat brushed against my leg.

"And how many exhausted American vagrants have you eaten recently?" I asked it. "I bet you've had that Swainson's. Was it tasty?" After being stroked and petted, it slunk off into the undergrowth, no doubt to cause grief to yet more cripplers.

At midday we decided we would slink off down to the Turk's Head ourselves. There was nothing further to report as we passed the queue at the Parsonage.

Over lunch we made the decision to abandon the Swainson's Thrush and go over to Gugh (pronounced goo) instead. It is a small island separated from St. Agnes, except at low tide when they are joined by a pebble causeway. It is almost as rarely visited by birders as St. Martin's and therefore had a distinct attraction for the Giant who was still determined to find his very own crippler.

We were relaxing happily in the sun, having finished an excellent prawn salad lunch washed down by an equally excellent pint when a birder rushed up announcing excitedly,

"The last lot who've just come out of the Parsonage saw the Swainson's; it showed at around half past twelve."

"We'd better go and see if we can get into the Parsonage, I suppose", said the Giant with little enthusiasm. He wasn't going to get his chance to locate his very own crippler after all. We headed for the Parsonage and joined the queue. Birders were being allowed one-hour stints. After we had waited half an hour, despondent birders shuffled out unenthusiastically.

"Did you see it?" we asked.

"One or two of us at the front did", one of them grumbled as he came out. "Hardly worth it though; all I saw was something brown dive into the bushes which could have been absolutely anything. In many ways, I wish I hadn't seen it, because I certainly can't tick it. I don't think any of the others at the front did that much better." We waited an hour while the next group went in. They were totally unsuccessful, and then it was our turn.

In we filed. We settled ourselves on the grass as quietly as possible, and then there was complete silence. In front of us the ground sloped gently away. A few feet from the people at the front, the first gnarled apple tree of the orchard blocked our view. The cover was so good, it was very difficult to see more than a few yards in any direction, and the whole orchard was surrounded by walls and dense hedges. I had managed to get one of the better spots as I had reasonable sight lines both to left and right. The time passed by with almost imperceptible slowness. Occasionally there was a slight rustle as someone tried to relieve the agonies of cramp. Someone struck a match in order to have a cigarette. The whole assembled company glared at him in disapproval. An immature Goldcrest appeared in a bush momentarily and a Melodious Warbler hopped around in the canopy above us, searching for insect larvae. Most of us were suffering from some degree of cramp by the time our hour had passed.

"Time's up", announced an organising birder in a loud whisper. Gratefully we stretched our legs as we stood up and shuffled out to let the next group in. Most of our lot wandered off down the road, but Brian and I decided to join the queue again and try for another go. After the next batch had gone in, there was still room for one or two more, so Brian and I went in for a second stint of suffering. The second hour was almost as uneventful as the first. Someone saw a brown bird in dense vegetation to the right which he thought might have been it. After the second hour we stood up with an urgent need to stretch our legs. When we emerged we bumped into Chris and Tessa.

"Any luck?" they asked.

"Not a chance", we replied. "And that's after a couple of hours."

"Well, you'll be lucky now we're here", said Chris with a confident smile, and we joined them reluctantly to file in a third time. We hadn't settled down for more than a few moments when our silence was rudely broken by the owner of the house next door returning home. The gate squeaked noisily on un-oiled hinges, and a dog barked its greeting.

"Do you want a cup of tea?" his wife asked cheerily. It seemed odd that outside the Parsonage orchard life continued unaffected by the Swainson's Thrush only a few yards away from us. It wasn't many minutes before silence descended on us all once again.

"The Swainson's Thrush is in the garden next door", someone announced coming down into the orchard from the gate. He made absolutely no attempt to lower his voice, and we all turned to face him. "It's in the middle of the lawn pulling up worms", he continued. There was an immediate shuffle of relief, followed by the beginnings of a scramble to the gate. "There's no point in leaving here and trying to see it", he added quickly. "There's only one hole in the wall you can see it from, and there's a bloke in front of it who's been waiting all day, and several behind him waiting desperately for a glimpse. You're much better off here, because the last I heard it was moving gradually in this direction."

We waited with renewed enthusiasm. It seemed incredible, but perhaps there was just the outside chance we might see this bird after all. It still came as a surprise when a tawny, brown bird the size of a Wheatear hopped up from nowhere onto a tree stump no more than five feet in front of me. It held its beak in the air at a tilt, giving it an air of haughty disdain. Moustachial stripes behind its beak added to its superior demeanour. It looked a lot like a Song Thrush except that the spotting on the breast was confined to a smaller area below the chin and was less conspicuous. The bird was also a less rich brown. It sat motionless on that stump for one long minute, maybe more.

"That's a Swainson's Thrush", I thought to myself as comprehension began to dawn. It cannot possibly be anything else. It seemed strange that there was absolutely no reaction from any of the stunned and silent birders around me. It certainly says a lot for their self control that no one even gasped. Thank goodness everyone had the presence of mind to realise that if anyone made the slightest noise or movement it would be gone. The views we were enjoying were crippling if not thoroughly stonking. After posing for us on the stump, it hopped up onto a branch of one of the apple trees for a second or two and then flew up into the higher branches of the oak trees above. The views on the stump were the best; all in all we probably watched it for at least ten minutes. These were certainly the best views anyone had had of this particular Swainson's Thrush so far. We left the Parsonage with a feeling of both relief and elation. Whether any more birders went into the Parsonage that afternoon I don't know; I rather doubt it. Most of the other birders who had visited St. Agnes that day had given it up as a bad job. We went down to the quay and took the boat back to St. Mary's.

We returned to hear the news that a Richard's Pipit, known to twitchers as either a Dick's Pip or Dicky Pipit, had turned up in a field near Normandy Farm, which is up in the north of the island. It's a long way, and at first we thought we would take a taxi. Taxis frequently ferry birders around St. Mary's at breakneck speed, crammed to the gunwales from one end of the island to the other after rare birds. However, the island bus was waiting in the square. It was much cheaper, so we took that. For the same small fare it will drop you off anywhere on its circular route.

When we arrived at Normandy Farm we heard that the bird was probably stringy. I have used this term before about a bedraggled Marsh Warbler, and its meaning is probably obvious. It means that the bird in question hasn't been looked at properly and is probably something very much more common than its finder proposes. Opinion seemed to be that it was just a rather large Meadow Pipit. We scanned the fields in the area on the off chance and then made our way through the lovely wooded valley of Holy Vale to Porth Hellick Pool. I was keen to see the Common Rosefinch again, and the others still hadn't seen the Solitary Sandpiper that was reported to have come back. I was unlucky with the Rosefinch, but we all had excellent views of the Solitary Sandpiper and managed to see the diagnostic lack of a white rump when it flew to another part of the pool. This feature is the best way of separating Solitary from the very similar, and much more common, Green Sandpiper.

While I was waiting in vain for the Rosefinch to appear, a Short-eared Owl flew low over the skyline above Porth Hellick Bay. This species is a good bird to see on the Scillies and is treated with especial enthusiasm by those, and that is most of us, who keep a Scilly list. There were quite a few birders watching it when it took it into its head to swoop down and land on a temporarily abandoned telescope. Imagine the surprise of its owner when he returned to collect it to be faced by a Short-eared Owl making eyes at him quizzically as it used his scope as a convenient perch.

Gradually the light began to fade. We had had an excellent day and were all feeling content as we made our way back to town, a drink and supper. Wickedly, Brian decided we ought to grip off Clive. A well-aimed grip off is one of the nastiest things that can hit any birder. Much worse than being hit by an eagle falling from the sky! Clive had placed himself in the firing line of the grip off of the century. Earlier I mentioned how I felt when Chris had gripped me off with his RB Flickers on the Garrison. That feeling pales into insignificance when compared with the feelings Clive would feel when gripped off with tales of the Swainson's Thrush.

Clive was the only one of our crowd who had suffered in the Parsonage for the Swainson's Thrush before. He had sat in its confined space when the weather was utterly foul. He had endured the extremities of suffering and got very wet; in fact, he had said he never wanted to see the wretched place again as long as he lived. However, he wanted to see that Swainson's Thrush as much as the rest of us, having invested hours of suffering probably even more. Weren't we nasty! Anyway, the Mega-grip off went something like this. It was stage-managed by Brian who was most unkind, but it is all very much part of the sport of Scilly birding.

We guessed that Clive would be sitting in the Mermaid by seven thirty. It was arranged that I should go in first, as he already knew I had intended to go to St. Agnes. There he was sitting at the bar talking to a group of his friends.

"Hello Clive", I greeted him cheerily. "How was St. Mary's today? See anything stunning?"

"Not a lot", he replied. "Didn't get to grips with the Richard's at Normandy, but then it was probably stringy anyway. Got excellent views of the Solitary Sand at Porth Hellick though. You haven't seen that properly yet, have you? How was St. Agnes and the Parsonage. Pretty boring I'd imagine, wasn't it...bloody hole!"

"Not exactly", I replied. "Spent the morning wandering about St. Agnes; there was an enormous queue for the Parsonage. Saw a very smart Melodious Warbler. Someone actually saw the Swainson's Thrush in the Parsonage at half past twelve, so after lunch I went and joined the queue. Spent an hour and a half hour in the queue to then spend an uncomfortable hour getting cramp in the Parsonage."

"I dunno", Clive crowed happily. "Some people will never learn. That Swainson's doesn't really exist. At least so long as it's taken up residence in the bloody Parsonage, it might just as well not do so as far as we birders are concerned."

"I even went in for a second unsuccessful hour."

"There's one born every minute!" Clive smirked smugly. He was beginning to enjoy himself as he had had the good sense not to waste his time on St. Agnes.

"Then I went in a third time", I continued. I think at this stage Clive must have begun to twig that something was up. I had after all been stringing out my story a bit, and I didn't seem to be quite as fed up as I ought to have been after such a wasted day. "I hadn't been in there long when the Swainson's Thrush hopped up onto a stump a few yards away. Had absolutely stonking views. All in all, those lucky enough to be in the Parsonage when at last it happened must have watched the bird for more than ten minutes."

"You didn't?" Clive was totally deflated. "You're having me on. You are, aren't you? Say you're having me on."

Five minutes later in came a smiling Chris, accompanied by Tessa.

"Hi there, Clive", Chris beamed. "How'd you get on today?"

"St. Mary's was pretty dull, actually", he replied. "How did you get on? Simon's been trying to kid me on he saw the Swainson's Thrush."

"Actually, we had our usual, lazy laid back morning", Chris replied casually. "Nothing much about on Mary's, so we thought we might as well go across to Aggie. Caught the two fifteen..."

"You didn't..." Clive spluttered, and had turned a few shades paler.

"We didn't what?" Chris smiled. "Well, we thought we might as well amble around Aggie for a bit, then we came across Simon at around three o'clock standing outside the Parsonage. Poor bugger had already wasted two hours in there." Chris was thoroughly enjoying himself; he was playing with Clive like a cat with a mouse.

"You didn't..." Clive spluttered a second time, now looking very uncomfortable indeed.

"I think Simon had had enough, but we thought we might as well give it a whirl, nothing to lose. In the end, Simon thought he might as well come in as well. After waiting less than ten minutes there it was. Landed just in front of us. Could have reached out and touched it! Still I expect Simon's told you all about it already, hasn't he?" By this time poor Clive was beginning to look really ill. At least Brian had spent the day on St. Martin's...or had he? Clive thought he might at least have one colleague in anguish, but the reprieve was short lived. The final, devastating thrust was seconds away, and the truth began to dawn as Clive noticed the broad grin which lit up Brian's face as he strode into the bar.

"Hi Clive", he beamed.

"Hello Brian", Clive replied weakly. "How was Martin's? Did you manage to find your crippler?"

"No!" the Giant replied, feigning disgust. "They wouldn't put on a boat...just for one. No one wanted to go to Martin's, except me. I had to go off to Aggie with Simon after the Swainson's instead. Had to wait more than two hours for it, but it was worth it. Got crippling views in the end." Poor Clive! But I suspect that had he or any one of us had the chance to do the same, we wouldn't have hesitated. In Scilly, despair is usually rapidly followed by euphoria. I wouldn't be surprised if the grip off that evening didn't make seeing the Swainson's Thrush all the sweeter for Clive. The next day he enjoyed views which were apparently quite as good as ours, if not better.

9. Two quiet days...it happens, even on Scilly

After the frenetic excitement of the Yellowthroat and the Swainson's Thrush, the next two days seemed very quiet. Apart from the stringy Richard's Pipit and the extremely elusive Dotterel and Common Rosefinch, there was nothing new to go for now.

Next morning the weather was absolutely superb, which is always a bad sign. It was very warm with brilliant, strong sunshine: quite extraordinary for October. The first thing I did was to wander down towards Porth Hellick Pool. I stood in line with about 50 other birders for at least three hours in the vain hope of catching a glimpse of the Common Rosefinch. At twelve thirty, after there hadn't even been a hint of it, I left as my stomach told me the need for lunch was pressing. I walked towards the northern end of the island and found a café at a place called Carne Veane. Here I had a very pleasant pint and ploughman's lunch sitting in a peaceful garden. Afterwards I went off in search of a place called Watermill Lane. There were several birders there when I arrived, but none had seen the Red-breasted Flycatcher, which had been reported. There was a rather smart flycatcher hopping about, but it had a distinctly spotty breast and not even a trace of white tail flashes.

Apart from news of a distant Great Northern Diver and Red-necked Grebe off a neighbouring bay, there was no further gen. I left Watermill Lane and took a narrow cliff top path, which led through open pine woods. There was a lovely resinous, late summer smell of pine needles that hung in the still afternoon air. The views of the other islands from this path were stunning; they reminded me strongly of similar views of the Hebrides in western Scotland. Land made brown by autumn tints contrasted strongly with the Mediterranean blue of the sea and sky. The air was crystal clear. In the far distance I could see the Cornish mainland quite clearly. Speckled Wood butterflies flitted lazily across my path. It was a glorious afternoon, and I thoroughly enjoyed my walk in spite of the total lack of any interesting birds.

After an hour or so of my own company, I came upon a more major road. I bumped into a few birders who were wandering listlessly, enjoying the late summer. There was still no news of anything, so I wandered back to Porth Hellick Pool to see if the Rosefinch had re-appeared. It hadn't. I spent another hour or so there of patient waiting...just in case. As it hadn't been seen all day, it did rather look as though it had gone. I went to have a look at the Solitary Sandpiper and witnessed it wandering into a reed bed and was not to be seen again. With nothing else to attract me in the ornithological line, I wandered slowly back to the Garrison.

That evening, the second annual Birders' Ball took place in the Porthcressa. People were encouraged to go in appropriate birdy costumes. One chap managed to make a rather fine headgear resembling an Ovenbird, but most didn't bother. An ovenbird is a large American warbler whose sole claim to fame at the time was that a corpse had been found in Britain just once. Later things got very boisterous, possibly because of the great scarcity of female birders. One chap got quite badly hurt. He landed on his head in the middle of the floor and bled dramatically. The lights went up and an ambulance was called, and that concluded the evening's entertainment. I saw the chap next day; he'd been stitched up in hospital. Apart from a rather thick and bandaged head, he seemed none the worse for wear.

The next day was just as quiet once an initial excitement had passed. I didn't even try to see any birds but spent the day in my own company studying lichens on Bryher. No new birds had been found for me to go for, as I discovered when I returned late in the afternoon. This was a relief in some ways, but on the other hand, some excitement would have been welcome for the next day, especially after two days of ornithological inactivity.

That initial excitement was indicated by a large group of birders I encountered on my way down to catch the boat for Bryher.

"What have you got?" I asked excitedly.

"Oh, nothing special", came the somewhat bored reply. "Just a couple of RB Flickers up in the pines", he added casually. My heart missed a beat. They weren't immediately apparent, at least not to me. I only had to wait a couple of minutes, however, before I caught sight of them hawking flies in the upper branches. They acrobatically hovered and darted about in the canopy, providing me with a great deal of pleasure. They flicked their tails as they hovered, thereby giving excellent views of their diagnostic white tail flashes. After the angst of the grip off at the beginning of the trip, it all seemed so easy. It dawned on me as I strolled on towards the boat that I had just enjoyed a very satisfactory tick. Feeling distinctly chuffed, I wandered on down to the quay and caught the boat to Bryher.

When we arrived at the quay on Bryher, most of my fellow passengers leapt off at high speed in pursuit of the Yellowthroat. Most were mainland birders who were making a special trip especially for this bird. Ahead of them were hours of boredom staring at a tree full of Golden Delicious. I felt smug and enjoyed a feeling of superiority; I had seen it! I thought it might be quite fun to see it again before exploring the island. I strolled along the shore to be greeted by a familiar scene. This time I lacked that feeling of high tension and drama, which is probably one of the main reasons for birding, if we only but knew it. A long distance birder was lying prone on the grass snoring softly to himself. The blissful, faraway expression on his face indicated that he had seen the bird. After a quarter of an hour or so I caught the briefest glimpse of the Yellowthroat as it dashed from one *Pittosporum* bush to another. There was a wave of excitement amongst the onlookers. For some, this brief moment would satisfy. Although unsatisfactory, it did constitute that all-important tick. I reminisced with immense pleasure on my experience of that fantastic little bird.

I left the Yellowthroat watchers to their vigil and enjoyed a few delightful hours studying the ancient heathland of Bryher on my own. Birds seemed miles away, and life was very peaceful and pleasant. Perhaps I needed a holiday from the frenetic tension of my first Scilly birding experience. I stood on isolated, craggy headlands, as wind, heavy with salt spray, was whipped up from the sea. I felt exhilarated, elated and gloriously at peace with the world.

Several hours later, I returned to the present reality of Scilly birding, feeling refreshed and invigorated. I passed the Yellowthroat vigil without stopping, made my way to the quay and the boat for St. Mary's.

Before supper that evening, the Giant and I took a pleasant stroll over Peninnis Head and enjoyed watching a Whimbrel stunningly close. On the way back, we were rewarded by breathtaking views of the sun setting in a glorious and flamboyant firework display over St. Agnes, the Bishop's Rock Lighthouse and the distant Islet of Annet. We wandered slowly into town as the light faded slowly and passed gently to evening. That evening, we enjoyed a fabulous meal in the Mermaid. The specialty of the house was Beef Stroganoff. It was a very illusive item and rarely available…but tonight it was on the menu.

10. More birds arrive in the Scilly Islands...at last

Looking at my notebook to see what was present in the Scilly Islands at that time, I found to my surprise that I had written just two rude words to sum it up. Bugger All! So when I set off the following morning, I had few expectations. First, as was now becoming a habit, I consulted the Porthcressa board. That was definitely more promising:

2 Dotterel	*Golf Course*
? Little Bunting	*St. Agnes*

I decided that, if the Little Bunting firmed up at all, I would go to St. Agnes in the afternoon. In the meantime, the golf course looked more than promising.

I walked determinedly along the coast road towards the golf course in high spirits. On the way I passed at least two groups of birders looking for Black Redstarts. There were several about, and this was definitely promising as it indicated an overnight arrival of new migrant birds. However, when I arrived at the golf course, there was an ominous lack of birders. Was I going to dip out yet again? I met two birders just leaving the course after which it seemed birder free.

"Any news on the Dotterel?" I asked anxiously.

"Yeah!" they replied casually. "They're up on the fairway just over the brow of the hill. No problem. There are two of them sitting together in the short grass."

I felt a pang of anxiety mingled with expectancy. Even now they were quite capable of flying off before I got there, especially if a helicopter flew in from the mainland. I arrived to find one or two birders with cameras, tripods and telephoto lenses looking very intently at the ground a very few yards in front of them.

I scanned the area, and to my delight the birds were sitting eight feet in front of the birding photographers at most. I walked carefully towards the birders and the birds in a wide arc so as not to disturb them. I crept as close as I dared but didn't get nearly as close as the birders already there. One of the birds was getting agitated, as was the birder photographing it. In my ignorance, I had inadvertently broken the skyline, and the sight of my silhouette had upset the birds. One of them ran a few yards, twitched its plumage a while, then settled down once more.

They were delightful birds. One was better marked than the other. It had the faintest remains of its summer plumage, which consists of a quartered chestnut area on the breast. I have come across few more confident birds. Whether they were aware of us and thought we were unaware of them, I do not know. They sat peacefully in the short grass, only shuffling occasionally if a birder got too close, and allowed themselves to be enjoyed and photographed. I had no telephoto lens with me, just a standard camera. To my surprise, the dot in the photograph is quite recognisable as a Dotterel. As time passed, more birders arrived. After a while, the Dotterel stood up, shuffled a few more feet across the turf only to sit down peacefully once more to continue waiting patiently for heaven knows what. I had had wonderful views of these delightful birds and decided it was time to leave.

As I walked around St. Mary's, there was still no definite news of anything. For something to do, I walked off in the direction of Normandy Farm on the off chance that the

Richard's Pipit might have been re-found. I didn't see a Richard's Pipit, but approaching Telegraph Hill just north of the golf course I began to hear reports.

"Two Short-toed Larks have just flown in the direction of Watermill Lane", announced a chap as he rode by on his bicycle. I passed a group of birders who were looking at one, possibly two Lapland Buntings in a field. They were proving to be very difficult to see as they were hiding in weed-covered furrows, and so I left. A few yards further on more birders were counting Black Redstarts in a hedge. Later at the evening log-in at the Porthcressa, a fantastic forty Black Redstarts were reported on St. Mary's. Already that day there was evidence of a fall. Exhausted, migrating birds had stopped for a breather on the Scillies on their migration route south. I wondered excitedly what rarities might be found as a result of this fall. There was an almost tangible excitement in the air, and this is what Scilly birding is all about.

I walked slowly along the road, again in the vicinity of Watermill Lane, in the hopes of seeing the Short-toed Larks. I heard later that a Tawny Pipit was found in the field just as I left the Lapland Buntings. The previous evening there had been rumours of a further Blackpoll Warbler. This was supposed to have been seen near to a pond between the Lapland Buntings and Watermill Lane. Meanwhile, close to the spot where the Blackpoll Warbler had been reported, I found a couple of birders peering into a small copse.

"What have you got?" I enquired.

"There's a rather nice Yellow-browed Warbler in the bushes", one of them replied. I leant softly on the drystone wall and peered through a gap in the hedge.

"Oh yes", I whispered after a few seconds. "Great!" I could see a Yellow-browed Warbler hopping about in the lower branches of a sycamore really close. "Oh dear! It's dived", I reported.

"Has it?" asked one of the other birders in disbelief. "Mine hasn't. I can still see it. It's on that straight branch, the one pointing to the left. Can't you see it?"

"No I can't", I replied. As it happened, he was looking at another bird which was even closer than mine had been. Eventually he managed to direct me onto it. In the end it turned out that there were at least three Yellow-browed Warblers in those bushes in front of us. He had seen two in his bush just before I had arrived and found mine.

I left the warblers, and it wasn't long before I came across another group of birders. At first, there were only two or three of them, but soon others joined us as it became apparent that something exciting was happening.

"What is it?" I asked eagerly.

"It could be that it's only a Blackbird", they replied. "But it's got this amazing bright red breast." We waited a minute or two.

"There it is!"

"Yeah! Got it", I replied. I could see a rather long tailed, russet breasted thrush, which did look pretty exciting. Somehow, but perhaps it was my over-vivid imagination, the back looked blue-black rather than black. The upper part of the throat seemed almost white and streaky. To me it also seemed more slender than a standard Blackbird. These could be the beginnings of a mega twitch, I thought to myself eagerly. As if by magic, the masses began to arrive from nowhere. One or two birders with CB radios began to report back to base.

"What is it?"

"Strange Blackbird, or something."

"Where?"

"Dunno."

"I've got it!"

"Where?"

"Two the right of the hawthorn bush with all the berries. Just above that dry stone wall."

"Got you...it's a Blackbird, isn't it? It's a bit bright, but I can't see why it's not just a juvenile Blackbird." It flew away.

"Anyone still on it?" someone asked. By this time the Blackbird, or whatever it was, had attracted at least fifty birders, and more were arriving by the second. Someone got out a book.

"How's about Dusky Thrush", he suggested excitedly.

"No, it can't be that, it's got a black vent", someone else observed, joining in the discussion.

"What the devil is it then?" The chap with the book looked puzzled. "Couldn't be a Yankee Robin, could it?" It appeared again, and suddenly it began to look less bright and exciting. Opinions passed backwards and forwards. Yet more birders arrived as a consensus was also arrived at.

"It's a Blackbird. Can't be anything else with that black vent. It's just rather odd, a juvenile Blackbird, that's all." One by one, feeling vaguely cheated and disappointed, birders began to move away. An amazing array of exotic thrushes were to arrive in the Scillies that autumn, but American Robin and Dusky Thrush were not amongst them. If Blackbirds had been rare, I rather doubt that that bird would have been accepted as one. It was an intriguing experience watching an identification develop.

I left the Blackbird and made my way through Holy Vale towards Porth Hellick Pool. However, this part of the island, which is normally so good, was not producing the goods today. I began to walk back towards the town and the Porthcressa in search of new gen. As I wandered around Old Town Bay I bumped into a birder who told me that a Short-toed Lark had been found up on Peninnis Head. I thanked him and dashed off eagerly. On the way up to Peninnis, I passed a small group of people.

"Any news of the Short-toed?" I asked anxiously. They regarded me with blank astonishment, as if I were deranged. They were having a picnic. After a few perplexing moments, the truth dawned on them.

"We're not birders", they muttered, as if this explained all. Just imagine for a moment that you are a normal human being, and I suppose, even if you are reading this account, this is a possibility. You're enjoying the country air and a pleasant picnic when this anxious fellow comes rushing up demanding information about a Short toad! I reckon you would have considered he had completely lost his marbles. Needless to say they couldn't help me, so I hurried on up to Peninnis Head. When I got there, feeling somewhat breathless from the ascent, I discovered a large crowd leaning over a drystone wall and staring into a freshly ploughed field. Someone told me where to look, and I was soon onto a rather fat, short-legged bird shuffling around in amongst a flock of House Sparrows. It was pale beige in colour. It had a stocky beak and streaky plumage. It was much paler and a little smaller than the average Skylark. Possibly it had shorter toes as well, but I have to admit I didn't notice. Why on earth it got itself called a Short-toed Lark and not something like a rather pale lark I cannot imagine.

When I had seen enough of the Short-toed Lark, I made my way down to the Porthcressa. The board informed me that the Little Bunting had been seen again on St. Agnes, but there was no indication as to how long, or when. I had a quick pasty and a coffee, and then left to catch the boat for St. Agnes.

I was about to learn another important rule of Scilly birding the hard way. It is best to avoid becoming an Island Hopper! This activity can be time consuming and a terrible waste of money. There is absolutely no point in going off to the other islands unless the information on the bird is good, and up to the minute. Once I had bought my ticket and was sitting in the boat, I heard the depressing news that the Little Bunting hadn't been seen since early morning. It had only been seen for a few seconds even then. There was not much indication that it was still on St. Agnes. I nearly got off the boat there and then as I had a sneaking suspicion I was on a fool's errand.

Once on St. Agnes, I walked up past the Post Office where the Blackpoll Warbler had been. There wasn't a soul there now. In one of the fields the cabbages had gone, and the field had been ploughed. However, that row of runner beans was still there which brought the memories flooding back. On this occasion, the bird I wanted to see was at the other end of the island in an area known as Troytown. This part of the island consists of a network of small, intimate bulb fields enclosed by tall *Pittosporum* hedges. On a hillside above these was an area of waste ground covered in bracken and very dense bramble. It was in this tangle that the Little Bunting had been reported. Early that morning, it had been seen to dive into the densest part of the thicket. The birders surrounding the tangle of vegetation looked tired and dispirited. A keen wind was blowing which made my eyes water. Identifying the birds, which were being blown in or out of that scrub, was impossible. It was all rather a waste of time. I was very relieved when a typical Scilly messenger arrived laden with news. Breathlessly he announced the latest gen.

"Arctic Warbler's turned up on Tresco", he announced. "Boat's leaving from the quay in ten minutes." Lingering on St. Agnes was obviously not going to be particularly profitable, so I joined the stampede down to the quay. When we arrived on Tresco, we made ourselves very hot and exhausted by running as hard as Barbours and boots would allow. The bird was reported to be on the opposite side of Great Pool. Unfortunately, we were all playing follow-my-leader! And ours took us the wrong way.

Eventually we did find the area of Tresco in question. As so often happens on these occasions, breathless birders arrived on the scene, puffing and panting noisily and demanding the latest information. This always makes the chances of seeing anything for at least quarter of an hour, if not for the rest of the day, improbable. I would like to make a simple proposal. I have no objection to birders running if they must, so long as they stop a hundred yards short of the site to get their breath back. There is little point in arriving while still puffing and panting like a steam engine. Secondly, they won't scare everything off for miles around with the racket from their herd-like, boot-clad feet. I have nothing against rushing from site to site if that's what birders really wish to do. It's good exercise amongst other things and an excellent antidote to all those pints in the pub. I do think that arriving noisily is completely daft, though. After all, everyone wants to see birds. However, no one will ever see anything, however fast they run, if they scare everything off simply by arriving.

On this particular occasion, the bird of the moment had been scared off something like an hour and a half before I arrived. The site was a narrow strip of willow scrub sandwiched between the main track-way and the lake. The path seethed and steamed with desperate and breathless birders who were puffing, muttering and shuffling. The light was fading fast. An occasional small grey warbler shot from one branch to another like a bullet, not lingering long enough to give any chance of identification. A few days later I heard that the supposed Arctic Warbler had been relocated that afternoon in the same willow scrub, but a few yards further down. Very few people saw it, and no one ever saw it properly. Eventually, the British Rarities Committee rejected the sighting.

It was now late afternoon, and I had spent quite a lot of money and had dipped on two birds. I was about to dip on a third.

The light had faded, making seeing the Arctic Warbler unlikely. I made my way back with the others to the quay. A boatload of disconsolate birders, many of whom had also wasted time on St. Agnes, made its way back to St. Mary's. When I got back, I hadn't walked far when I heard about the third bird. A Red-rumped Swallow had been found up by the Longstones Centre in the middle of the island. Richard Millington, author of *Twitcher's Diary*, who has since become synonymous with *Birdline*, was amongst that evening's dippers. At least I was in experienced company. As soon as he heard the news, he rushed to a telephone box and ordered a taxi. I hesitated for a while and, as they say, he who hesitates is lost. It really was getting very dingy.

After wasting precious time dithering and making up my mind, I decided I would rush off and try and see this bird. Reports from the returning birders were promising, but there were very few heading in the same direction as me, still on their way to Longstones. All those returning to town had happy faces and talked of the crippling views they had had. The first ones I passed reported that it had gone to roost in a pine tree but was still very easy to see. As I approached Longstones I heard that it had taken a late evening flight and was now swooping over the heads of those still there. I was only a hundred yards or so from the site when the taxi carrying Richard Millington and others

It's all happening! Decisions...where is the best place

arrived, so I had lost little by going there on foot. I got to the site to hear that, although it had been flying around the trees a minute beforehand, it had temporarily disappeared.

Minutes passed and with them any chance of seeing the bird. Ordinary Barn Swallows could be seen flying high over Holy Vale, but in this light they were indistinguishable from bats, let alone other interesting kinds of swallows. It soon became apparent that even if the bird were to return to one of the closest pines, it would have been unrecognisable in the dark. I gave it up as a bad job and walked disconsolately back to town.

I went into the Mermaid and was confronted by Clive with a happy smile on his face.

"Did you see that Red-rumped Swallow?" he beamed enthusiastically. "Wasn't it a beauty!"

"No I didn't", I replied.

He proceeded to tell me all about the stunning views he had had. He was getting his own back for the Swainson's Thrush, and he knew it. Three other members of the Christchurch Harbour Ornithological Group arrived on Scilly that day which completed our party. These were all Scilly birders of considerable standing, the sort who could do enviable things like identifying birds as they flew overhead on the characteristics of a single cheep. They were in a different league as far as I was concerned. Imagine my sense of shame when I went down to the Mermaid after I had had my supper and admitted to them that I had done a silly! I had wasted a lot of money and had somehow managed to dip on three good birds. I felt like creeping off into a little corner as I was certain to be the subject of derisive laughter. In fact, the others were surprisingly sympathetic. Chris and Tessa generously admitted that they would almost certainly have done exactly the same under the circumstances. The recently arrived Choggers were scornfully amused. They were serious birders and definitely disapproved of anything that smelt like a twitch.

In spite of the rather depressing second half of the day, things were definitely looking more promising than they had for some time. Whereas my diary had been depressingly negative recently about birds present on the Scillies, this evening it was different. The list of potential birds reported at the Porthcressa Log read as follows:

1-2 Lapland Buntings	*Telegraph Hill*
1-2 Short-toed Larks	*Telegraph Hill, Peninnis*
1-2 Richard's Pipits	*Telegraph Hill*
1-3 Little Buntings	*St. Agnes*
1 Arctic Warbler	*Tresco*
1 Red-rumped Swallow	*Longstones Centre*

1 Possible Red throated Pipit	*Tresco*
1 Woodchat Shrike	*St. Agnes*
1 Bluethroat	*Peninnis Head*
1 Bittern	*Locality unknown*

This was a healthy and encouraging situation with a very good number of potential ticks about. Reports suggested that the Little Bunting on St. Agnes had been joined by a second and possibly even a third. A Red-throated Pipit had been heard calling over the helicopter pad on Tresco, and a juvenile Woodchat Shrike had also arrived on St. Agnes. A Bluethroat had been seen briefly amongst dense vegetation on Peninnis Head, and there were some vague rumours of a Bittern. It did look as though tomorrow might be quite an exciting day.

11. Return to St. Agnes...and yet more fine weather

The next day Brian and I returned to St. Agnes. It was another beautiful day. The weather was brilliant with blue skies, and a strong sun shining down on us. It was the Little Buntings that we most wanted to see, so we walked down to the far end of the island to Troytown and the small bulb fields surrounded by *Pittosporum* hedges. Half way there and fairly close to the Post Office, we came across a small crowd looking at a small, raised plot filled with tree mallow. Hopping amongst the tree mallow and totally oblivious of its admirers was the Blackpoll Warbler. It had taken up permanent residence in this little plot where it had found an abundance of juicy caterpillars which were very much to its liking. There was no comparison between these views and the ones I had had when I first saw it. Rare birds which attract large numbers of admirers often become quite tame, and it is worrying to think what happens to these trusting creatures once they leave the comparative safety of the Scillies. I watched this little bird at leisure, and Brian made absolutely sure I admired its rather amazing yellow feet.

We wandered down in the direction of Troytown. A large crowd had assembled by the time we arrived, and there was excitement in the air.

"Any news on the bird?" I asked a birder casually.

"Which bird?" he asked enigmatically.

"What do you mean?" I replied. "The Little Bunting's the bird everyone's come to see, isn't it?"

"Not necessarily", he replied. "One or two people saw a Dusky Warbler a few moments ago flitting in and out of the

Pittosporum." A Dusky Warbler is a rare bird from Central Asia and potentially far more important to most of the assembled company. We waited for a few moments before we heard the now familiar sound of running boots as birders dashed off round the corner to another field.

"For goodness sake stop running!" someone shouted desperately. "You'll scare everything away." Although to stop running under such circumstances would be a laudable idea, it would be just too altruistic for most birders. By the time they got to the viewing point, it would be blocked by a crowd five or six people deep.

Off to see the Little Bunting on St. Agnes

I've already mentioned that Brian was no dwarf, and I'm over six foot tall; we didn't amble. In spite of our potential height advantage, we had a job to find a space in the line where we could see any of the field. The field in question was bounded by a hawthorn hedge. We peered as best we could between the rows of heads. The field in front of us had held a crop once but was now overgrown with weeds. These included thistles and other plants which provide seed attractive to birds. A flock of Goldfinches twittered happily as they tweaked the thistle heads for food. The field was actually full of birds. There were House Sparrows galore and several kinds of warbler, including Blackcap, busily feeding on the insects and seeds. It wasn't very long before a Little Bunting hopped up to feed on seeds from a thistle head. It was an attractive little bird, very like a slightly smaller version of a female Reed Bunting. Its head was attractively marked with chestnut patterns. After we had been there for ten minutes or so, it became apparent that there were two of them in the field. Although I never did see them together, one had better rich brown markings on the head than the other.

When the excitement of seeing the Little Buntings had died down a bit, I noticed a warbler that seemed darker than usual. It was hopping about on the ground close to where I had first seen the Little Buntings. There were some rather dark Chiffchaffs about. Let's be honest, I didn't have the faintest idea what a Dusky Warbler looked like. A few hours later, I met a lady birder who had been with us at the time on St. Agnes.

"How did you get on today?" I asked her.

"Oh, I've had a great day", she replied. "I was one of the few who saw the Dusky Warbler on St. Agnes. While everyone else was looking at those Little Buntings, it was hopping around the *Pittosporum* at the other end of the field. I actually saw it hop into the field out of the *Pittosporum*. Then it disappeared for a moment or two, and I saw it fly to the left and land amongst the weed down the other end."

This was the part of the field I had been looking at when I saw my dark warbler. Had I seen the Dusky Warbler? For a few moments I tried to convince myself that perhaps I had. However, I had not seen any obvious eye-stripe, a feature that I now knew was important. In fact, apart from it being darker than usual, I had seen no characters to confidently distinguish it from a Chiffchaff. Reluctantly, I had to admit that I didn't have that extra tick. Sadly, my very thin observations of my warbler were stringy to say the least.

Back at the field on St. Agnes, no one seemed to want to move, even after looking at the Little Buntings uncomfortably for half an hour. This was in spite of the fact that somewhere there was still a potential Dusky Warbler to be found. Brian and I left the Little Buntings and began to scrutinise all the smaller fields in the area. Very slowly we began to make our way towards the Parsonage. There were prodigious numbers of common warblers about, all darting busily in and out of the *Pittosporum*. Surely there just had to be something rare in amongst them. After a while, we bumped into a small group of birders ambling down towards Troytown. They walked a little faster when we told them that a couple of Little Buntings were down there and showing well. In turn, they told us that the juvenile Woodchat Shrike had been re-located and where we could see it. In fact, it wasn't much further along the path we were on.

Soon we saw a small crowd silhouetted against the skyline on a hillside in front of us. When we caught up with them we were just in time to hear that the Woodchat Shrike had hopped down behind a dry stone wall. However, we didn't have to wait very long before the bird hopped back up again. It was little more than a brown dot through my binoculars, but I could see that its behaviour was typical of a shrike. It perched conspicuously on the top of the same spiky bush before diving on some unsuspecting insect. After a while it flew closer, and I could see it had a more or less uniform, scaly brown plumage. It was a dull bird compared with the many adult birds I had seen perched on telegraph wires in Spain. Even though for me this was a new British bird, I found it hard to become particularly excited by it.

There were an astonishing number of butterflies and day flying moths about. We saw Red Admirals, Large and Small Whites, Small Tortoiseshells, as well as the occasional Holly Blue butterfly. Silver Y moths hovered busily in the fields made golden with Corn Marigold. Several different kinds of colourful hoverflies flitted from flower to flower. The scene was typical of August, but this was mid-October. We made our way towards the Parsonage. I was keen to see that place again as I had heard that a rare Cornish plant was growing there. I didn't find the plant, but I did see a superbly marked Red-breasted Flycatcher which I enjoyed at leisure. Since this was only my third, I was delighted. I had found the bird for myself, and I had the Parsonage to myself. It was in strange contrast to the time, just a day or two previously, when one had had to queue to get in. Now that the Swainson's Thrush had gone it was deserted.

I left the Parsonage and went off in search of Brian. I found him, and we headed towards the Turk's Head for lunch. We were enjoying a couple of succulent crab sandwiches and a pint when a boat arrived from St. Mary's. We could see Chris, Tessa, Leon and Bob in it. They were obviously going to try their luck with the Dusky Warbler, as all four of them had seen Little Buntings on many occasions.

I decided to leave St. Agnes, since I wanted to have another go for the Red-rumped Swallow. Just before we arrived back on St. Mary's, news came through on a CB radio that a Rustic

Bunting had turned up. The report of the bird wasn't far away, being beside the road up to the golf course. When I got there I found a tarmac entrance blocked by a gate. The entrance was twenty feet wide at most. On the gate was a conspicuous 'Private' notice. Birders were standing more than six deep in the hopes of seeing something beyond. Unfortunately, the ground sloped up to the gate so only those in the front row had any chance of seeing anything.

The bird had last been seen just beyond the gate on the road verge and had hopped over into the field. As it seemed a lost cause, I wandered on towards the Longstones Centre in the hopes of news of the Red-rumped Swallow. In the field opposite the one where the Rustic Bunting had disappeared, a Little Bunting had been reported. Two or three birders were giving the field a casual once over. There may have been several Little Buntings in the islands, but they are still pretty scarce birds, and I was astonished at how little interest this bird was attracting.

When I arrived at Longstones, and the area beneath the pines where everyone had been standing the previous evening, there was not a soul to be seen. What had happened to all those others who had dipped the previous evening? I scanned unsuccessfully for twenty minutes or so and then walked back to Longstones where I found a small group of birders relaxing over a cup of tea.

"Have you heard anything of the Red-rumped Swallow recently?" I asked desperately.

"Yeah", they replied casually. "It was just here...just a moment or two ago. A Merlin came over and chased it off; it disappeared in a flock of other swallows. Why, haven't you seen it yet?"

"No, I haven't", I replied testily. It could have gone anywhere by now. "Damned Merlin!" I muttered as I left them.

I had actually seen that Merlin from where I had been standing; I had even seen the swallows it had chased away. No doubt one of those black specks must have been the Red-rumped Swallow. I lingered for a short while in the general area. Birders rambled past from time to time and asked me what I was looking for.

"The Red-rumped Swallow!" I replied.

"Haven't you caught up with that yet?" they chuckled scornfully as they went by, shaking their heads in disbelief. It began to feel as though I was the only one left in the islands who had yet to see this bird. I examined all the birds flying around the pines as carefully as possible; there was a Sand Martin amongst them. This was a bird I had not seen before on the trip, but none had the pale pink rump of the bird I was now desperate to see.

After a further half hour, I was becoming increasingly impatient both with myself and with the bird. I walked down through Higher Moors in the direction of Porth Hellick. On occasions, it had also been reported down there. On the way, I heard that an Ortolan Bunting had been seen near Carne Friars, a cottage close to Porth Hellick Pool. I found the cottage, but there was neither sign of the bird, nor birders looking for it. I returned to Longstones yet again, realizing I really had no idea what to do next. Apparently, this was the favourite haunt of the bird as well as its roosting site. It seemed logical that if I waited there it must return sometime. When I approached Longstones I heard the news that it was now flying around Porthloo Pool, which was not far from the road to the golf course, close in fact to the field with the Rustic Bunting.

I shot off towards Porthloo Pool at a brisk pace but with little optimism. I was pretty convinced that by the time I got there it would have flown back to Longstones. To my total astonishment, I was joined by one or two birders who were in the same boat and still yet to see the Red-rumped Swallow. Telegraph wires by the roadside were crowded with migrating swallows, but none had the necessary red rump. As we approached Porthloo Pool we were told that it was currently flying around a group of pines viewable from a gateway close by. We approached the gateway, and after a few seconds the Red-rumped Swallow shot past the top of one of the pines at the speed of a bullet. I saw it just long enough to catch the pink band on its rump. I stood in front of the gate for some time, watching the tops of those pines. The bird flashed past quite frequently but never lingered long enough for me to get a really good view.

I left the pines after a while and walked down towards the sea, which was quite close. I was astonished at how many Sanderling were on the beach. Many were roosting, but others were rushing frantically towards the sea as a wave retreated, only to rush back up the beach again as the next wave approached. Somehow they never got wet, but, amazingly, despite expending so much energy, the small scraps of food they managed to pick up made it worthwhile. They looked like little clockwork toys.

So another good day's birding was approaching its end. I went off to the Mermaid in search of supper. That night there were reports of several new birds from the Log at the Porthcressa. New birds, apart from those already mentioned, were as follows:

Siberian Stonechat	*1 Gugh*
2 Tawny Pipits	*Airport*
Grey-headed Wagtail	*Peninnis Head*
Dusky Warbler	*Tresco*
Calandra Lark	*A vague rumour*

12. Back to Tresco...this time a much more successful visit

The best bird on the Scilly Isles was now definitely the Dusky Warbler...or perhaps one should say Warblers! I was also a bit keen to see a Tawny Pipit. I had seen these birds several times before, but always abroad. They constituted a UK tick! As far as the Dusky Warblers were concerned, I decided that the best thing to do was to wait until lunchtime, at least. By then there should be news as to whether either or both were showing well. This would give me a chance to go up to the airport to see the Tawny Pipit... or Pipits. On the way to the airport, I encountered a couple of aged gents carrying cameras; they didn't look like birders, although they were obviously searching for something.

"Say mate", they asked as I passed. "Which one of them bungalows is Harold Wilson's?" I hadn't a clue, but it amused me to think that there was more than one kind of twitcher on the islands.

I found the Tawny Pipit easily when I arrived at the Airport. There was a convenient group of birders obviously watching it. However, there was only one now as the second had left. There weren't that many people there, as most birders reckoned they had more important birds to see. While watching the Tawny Pipit, I met two birders of whom I was going to see quite a lot of during the next day or two. One was called John, the other Tim. John was a great enthusiast and an impressive source of information which he gave to all and sundry as he passed. There had been recent reports of a well-marked Common Rosefinch with a hint of green in its plumage. It had been flying amongst a flock of Linnets in waste ground close to Salakee Farm, not far from the Airport. We found a typical field full of seed-producing weeds and covered with finches; most were Linnets, but there appeared to be no Rosefinch amongst them. We went down to Porth Hellick and up to the Longstones Centre but saw nothing special.

At the Longstones Centre, there was news of an Ortolan Bunting at a place called Rocky Hills, yet another area of the Scillies I had never heard of. Luckily, it wasn't very far away. John told everyone about the Ortolan Bunting as our paths crossed, and soon we had a following like the Pied Piper of Hamelin.

The bird was in a cropped field. There was a track way running past the field which was bounded by a high bank, topped by a sycamore hedge. Getting any sort of a view through that hedge was tricky. I squeezed my way into the hedge and stared through a small hole in it. This bird turned out to be yet another that had been seen ten minutes before, but not since. A flock of sparrows was flying about, sometimes landing and feeding for a few moments. It wasn't too long before the Ortolan Bunting was re-located. Unfortunately it had flown down to the other end of the field, far too distant to allow a decent view. I had just found the correct flock of sparrows and located one that looked slightly different when they all flew back up into the hedge. Luckily a few moments later, the flock began to fly back down into the field, and this time a lot closer. It wasn't long before someone had relocated the Ortolan Bunting. The bird must have been obscured from my view by a branch, because, try as I might, I just couldn't see it. This was frustrating, as an Ortolan Bunting would be yet another lifer for me. It was also supposed to be very close. Eventually the chap nearest me realised I really couldn't see it from where I was and let me have a look through his gap; and there it was. It was a male with a well marked, grey head and a very pronounced white eye-ring.

After the three of us had seen it well, we walked into town to get some lunch and see what the latest news was on the Dusky Warblers. At the Porthcressa we heard that the St. Agnes bird was being very difficult, but at that very moment on Tresco a chap with a CB was actually looking at one. This was certainly very encouraging. As there was no other significant news, the three of us decided to take the boat to Tresco that afternoon.

When we arrived, it was another sprint across the coastal heath and over the heliport to the other side of the island. Those who were with me agreed with my principle of walking the last few yards. This time the crowd was truly enormous. There must have been more than five hundred birders there. Some were waiting in a track way leaning against a dry stone wall. Most were standing in a crescent on the edge of a maize field. Reports indicated that the bird had been seen at the back of the field, but not since the crowds had arrived. We were told that just an hour previously it had been flitting and calling freely all over the field and in the hedge beyond.

Those in front of the dry stone wall didn't have much chance of seeing anything if the bird did return, but to go into the field one was asked to contribute 50p to the *Save the Children Fund*. I paid my 50p gladly and went on in.

Inside, no one had the foggiest clue as to what was going on. I had an excellent view of the maize field, but unless this bird was a real exhibitionist, and from all I'd heard about Dusky Warblers the reverse seemed to be true, the chances of seeing it again were very poor indeed. I hadn't been waiting very long when someone in the corner of the field and on the far side of a hedge started signalling surreptitiously. He was pointing downwards and putting his other forefinger to his lips, indicating the need for secrecy. A few left the field very quietly, trying to draw as little attention to themselves as possible. I saw Richard Millington join them and so decided to see what was going on. I joined only a dozen other birders who were looking down a track way behind a gate. As I am tall I squatted down so that those behind me could get some sort of a view; it was most uncomfortable.

Waiting patiently for an elusive bird.

"Ssssh!... It's in the hedge to the right...moving this way", a man whispered urgently but scarcely audibly. "I can hear it. If we keep really quite we just might see it." After a moment or two, we could hear it calling quite clearly. It made a harsh tack...tack...tack sound.

"There it is", someone whispered above my left shoulder. "Halfway down the third sycamore on the right." I could see a small bird and, after wasting precious seconds on it, realised it was a Dunnock. I searched and searched. Apparently everyone else could see it except me. It was the same situation I had been in with the Ortolan Bunting all over again. I can only think that a sycamore leaf was obscuring my view. I couldn't move; there just wasn't room. A few moments later, the bird shot across the track and into a bush on the other side. I saw it fly across and sitting in the bush for a split second before it disappeared into denser cover. Few, if any birders would consider the views I had had as tickable.

Immobile and silent we waited a while longer, but it was soon apparent that it had gone. There was no tack…tack…tack; and this was a call it gave constantly. As I was feeling dreadfully uncomfortable I left my vantage point and joined the rest in the maize field. I spotted Chris and Tessa and went across to join them.

"Seen it yet, Simon?" Chris asked.

"Sort of", I replied. "Hardly what you would call tickable views, though." I realised that the bird had probably been too disturbed that afternoon for there to be any really decent view for anyone. I decided to go back to St. Mary's and try again the next day. After all, something could well have turned up there.

"Can you do a spot of shopping for us?" Tessa asked.

"Sure", I replied. I hoped to get a boat back at around three o'clock. I walked back to the quay at Great Grimsby to find a boat loaded with birders without room for me. It pulled out and was soon replaced by another, with a dozen or so birders waiting boarded.

"They won't be going till this boat's full", someone observed depressingly after we'd already waited twenty minutes.

It was another hour before we left. I wasn't exactly pleased. I could have spent that time much more profitably trying to get better views of the Dusky Warbler. To rub salt into the wound, we had to go via Bryher to pick up the few people who still needed to see the Yellowthroat. On the way back, the sea was quite choppy, and there was quite a bit of spray about. One poor bloke had been on Bryher all day making an unsuccessful attempt to see the Yellowthroat. To add insult to injury, he was sitting in the worst possible part of the boat and was getting utterly soaked every time we hit a wave. Strangely enough he seemed very cheerful and philosophical about it all. When eventually we arrived back at St. Mary's, I went to the supermarket to find it shut.

As it happened, things couldn't have turned out better for me, as I was about to discover. It was a little like having a big win on the lottery, although there was no such thing as a lottery in those days. After failing to get Chris and Tessa's shopping, I thought it best to go up to Greystones as quickly as possible to tell the others I had been unable to get their supper. On the way up the hill, I met three birders coming down the other way. They stopped to give me the gen.

"There's a Rustic Bunting up on the Garrison", they told me. "It's in the corner of the playing fields."

"Thanks", I replied and started to rush off as they called me back.

"Hold on a tick, don't you want to know where it is?" they asked.

I was a bit puzzled by this because I imagined that the crowd looking at it would make it immediately obvious where it was or, perhaps I should say, had been. The little experience I had had so far of Rustic Buntings led me to believe they were extremely shy birds. If there were many up there, I had very little chance of seeing it.

"How big's the mob?" I asked. "Won't I be able to tell where it is from them?" I could hardly believe my luck when they replied, "There's no one there. We found it ten minutes ago." They quickly told me exactly how to find it. "There was no one about to tell, so we're off to the Porthcressa to let them know. For the next ten minutes or so you should have it all to yourself."

"That's amazing", I said, as the wonderful truth dawned. "Thanks a lot." This is the sort of situation everyone dreams of on Scilly. I suppose it would have been fractionally better had I found it for myself, but I was about to see a very pretty and difficult bird in the peace and quiet of my own company. I made my way at a brisk pace to the top of the hill and crossed the playing fields. Ever so carefully I peered over the wall into the field in which it had been seen. There was a flutter of wings as a flock of sparrows, which had been ever so close, flew up into a hedge. I waited as quietly as I knew how, scarcely daring to breathe. After a moment or two, the first sparrow dropped back into the field followed by another, and another. The seventh or eighth bird to join the feeding flock looked very different. There it was, the Rustic Bunting, just a few yards away. It had a large, well-marked, almost box-shaped head and seemed larger than the sparrows. Its demeanour was more crouching and reminded me of a Skylark. The rusty red patches on the breast were easy to see, but I must admit I had expected it to have cleaner, whiter under parts. This was fantastic. I was looking at this little stunner all by myself without the hassle of any other birders. This Rustic Bunting was a bird that many people would give a lot to see, and, for the moment at least, it was all mine. I knew I didn't have much time because, in a moment or two, all hell would break loose.

With great care, I backed away from the wall. As soon as I was clear, I dashed the few yards across to Greystones to tell the others. I bashed on the door and found the three recent arrivals there.

"There's a Rustic Bunting in the corner of the playing fields", I announced breathlessly. As I have mentioned before, I was pretty new to this birding lark. Their first reaction to my news was that I was suffering from a dose of Scilly over-enthusiasm. No one moved. However, they decided to give it a try when I told them the full story and that everyone on St. Mary's would be there at any minute. I warned them about the skittishness of the flock, but, in spite of using utmost caution, the whole flock flew up into the hedge again. This time the Rustic Bunting landed just a little bit further way. The four of us enjoyed it for five minutes at most before suddenly, and breathlessly, the first birder from the Porthcressa arrived.

"Where's... this Rus...tic Bun...ting? ... pant... pant... pant", he gasped.

"It was there with a flock of sparrows, just ten yards away", I answered. "But I'm afraid you arrived and scared it off. It's flown down the hill and more or less out of sight." After some diligent searching, we located the sparrows, which were now little more than brown flecks, and just made out the Rustic Bunting amongst them. The field sloped steeply away from us, and the vegetation was much coarser lower down. The Rustic Bunting was now very hard to see, and people were climbing onto the wall that I had peered over so carefully about twenty minutes previously.

I knew that I had had the best views of anyone and glowed with an inner satisfaction. Chris and Tessa arrived on the scene.

"Seen it, Simon?" asked Chris.

"Yes I have, utterly crippling views", I replied

enthusiastically. "I had it all to myself ten minutes ago down to about five yards. It's somewhere down at the bottom of the field now though, I'm afraid."

"I know", Chris muttered irritably. "I saw it's head pop up from behind a clump of grass just now, but with this lot here we're never going to see it well. Looked a nice, well-marked bird."

"It was", I replied.

"You're bloody lucky, Simon", he went on. "You know that. Talk about jam!"

A good two hundred birders were now milling around in the corner of the playing fields or standing on top of the wall. Clive and the Giant arrived. Brian being tall managed to get one distant glimpse. To make matters worse, it was just beginning to get dark. The little flock now flew up, over the brow of the hill and out of sight. As the gloom intensified, a few saw what they thought was the bird fly off towards the Garrison campsite. A very few went off in the hopes of relocating it, but the majority drifted back down towards the town, determined to get up early and try first thing next morning.

I walked down to the Mermaid. That evening I had the opportunity to grip off most of the birders on St. Mary's. I could have been utterly unbearable and would have deserved a very cold dip in Porthcressa Bay! When I arrived at the Mermaid I made the decision to have a Beef Stroganoff to celebrate if it was on the menu. It was, and it was excellent!

According to the news, which filtered through from the Porthcressa log, very little that was new had turned up. Tomorrow I wanted to see that Dusky Warbler on Tresco properly. After seeing the Rustic Bunting if it was still there, practically everyone on St. Mary's would want to go off to see one of the Dusky Warblers. By lunchtime, there could be an awful lot of bored birders wanting to leave Tresco or St. Agnes. If, by any good fortune, something crippling turned up on another island, they would want to leave Tresco or St. Agnes as fast as the first available boat would take them. Even better, the crippler just might turn up on St. Mary's, and I might be able to get it UTB before the Dusky Warbler crowd returned. If things worked out really well, I could perhaps enjoy the Dusky Warbler with a select few in the afternoon.

13. Plans that go like clock work... perhaps this is the Scilly answer?

At six o'clock the next morning I was woken by the sound of boots hammering past just outside the bungalow; dawn had scarcely broken. They're at it already! I thought smugly, meaning the desperate birders outside trying for the Rustic Bunting. Waves of boots in a desperate hurry pounded past. I wonder if they're onto it, I mused with glorious detachment and went back to sleep again peacefully to dream of further cripplers. It must have been eight o'clock when I woke again. I got dressed and walked across the dew-carpeted playing fields to the remnants of the Rustic Bunting crowd.

"Any luck?" I enquired.

"Naaa", they replied. "No chance! I reckon it's long gone. I heard some lucky bastard had it all to himself yesterday evening, then the crowds turned up and that was that."

"Anyone seen it this morning?" I asked, deciding not to be drawn into the temptation of admitting that I was that lucky bastard.

"Not here", they replied. "It could have popped up somewhere else, I suppose." There were to be two more Rustic Buntings that autumn. Both were on Tresco, and both were typical ploughed-field skulkers. At least people did get another chance. I wandered back to Greystones and prepared myself a fry up. Then I got ready and left for the Porthcressa where there was nothing to report yet. There was little else to do, so I went and had a look at the Scilly Isles Museum. It is well worth a visit by any visiting birder. There are historic specimens like the Eskimo Curlew, one of the very few ever to have graced our shores. This is a species which is on the verge of extinction worldwide. If one were to arrive on the Scillies today, at least it would not get shot! Instead it would give immense pleasure to hundreds of birders. There is a good range of other rarities which are preserved in recognisable condition. The collection of cased birds, donated by the Dorian Smith family, the owners of Tresco, is well worth a look. These are excellent examples of the taxidermist's art. If for no other reason, I reckon all visiting birders to the Scillies should pay their respects to this British Eskimo Curlew. There have been none in Britain since 1880 for which there are four records, all in the nineteenth century.

I wandered back to the Porthcressa to find that there was one new report; a possible Pallas's Warbler had turned up at Porth Hellick. I also bumped into John.

"What are you doing today, then?" I asked.

"I'm off to see the Short-toed Lark up at Longstones", he announced. "Then I'll probably go off to Tresco to try for the Dusky Warbler. Short-toed Lark is a lifer for me, so that has to come first."

"I saw the one on Peninnis a day or two ago", I added. "I reckon I'm going off to investigate this possible Pallas's. Trouble is how on earth can you have a possible Pallas's? They have to be one of the most obvious warblers there are."

"Pallas's Warblers are a bit like an ornithological firework display", John agreed, exaggerating perhaps just a tiny bit. "You start counting the stripes on any part of their anatomy, and once you're past three you know you've got a Pallas's." We went off together, but at Longstones we took our separate ways. After I had seen my Pallas's, and he had ticked off his Short-toed Lark, we agreed to meet back at Longstones, have coffee and go and have another look at the Ortolan Bunting; there were two of them in that field now. I hadn't left John for more than a minute or two when I bumped into four birders coming up the road from the direction of Porth Hellick. They treated me to one of the best examples of twitcher's jargon I have ever heard.

"Any news on this Pallas's?" I enquired.

"Complete ball of string!" one of them replied. "I wouldn't waste any of yer precious on it. First thing this morning, this conservation moosh got on 'is bike, didn't he? Then he peddles his way past Watermill Lane and strings an Olivaceous (warbler). Not content with that, he peddles off down to Porth Hellick and strings a Pallas's. That's either got to be the most incredible luck...or the largest ball of string you've ever seen. I favour the latter misself. To make it even more stringy, this moosh then has to look at the pictures in a book in the 'Cressa before he worked out what he'd had. Just has to be a complete ball of string. It's obvious! The Pallas's was just a juv. Firecrest. There's been one on the footpath to Porth Hellick Pool for a day or two. Can't think what he strung the Olivaceous from though. Chiffchaff probably."

I thanked them and went off to try and find John with his Short-toed Lark. When I found him, he was with his friend Tim amongst a group of a dozen birders. The Short-toed Lark was very close, and I enjoyed a really good look at it through John's telescope. This wasn't such a pale bird as the Peninnis one, nor so well marked. The general opinion was that they were two different birds. We were just about to go and have a look at the Ortolan Buntings when a chap arrived on his bicycle with a CB in his hand.

"That Olivaceous is gen after all", he announced. "It's been relocated and confirmed."

"Where?" we asked anxiously. An Olivaceous Warbler would cause an even greater stir than the Dusky had done. It had only been seen in Britain a handful of times before, and this was the first to have occurred for several years.

"Along the far end of Watermill Lane", he replied and peddled off to give others the good news. It wasn't very far to Watermill Lane, so I suggested we all shot off up there as quickly as possible. Very few birders anywhere would have had the opportunity to twitch an Olivaceous Warbler, and the eventual stampede would be extreme. In fact, it was to make a bigger stir that autumn than the Swainson's Thrush, although the Yellowthroat probably remained the star of the year.

The majority of the birding population of the Scilly Isles was currently on Tresco, trying for the Dusky Warbler. This Olivaceous Warbler was exactly the sort of bird which would clear Tresco. Things were working out very nicely indeed. On the way up to Watermill Lane we picked up other birders as John gave out the news.

I was astonished at just how many birders had managed to congregate in Watermill Lane when we got there in spite of the Dusky Warbler on Tresco. Among them I recognised the tall figure of the Jolly Green Giant.

"What's the latest gen on this Olivaceous Warbler then, Brian?" I asked.

"I haven't seen it yet", he replied. "Evidently, it was last seen ten minutes ago. It was somewhere up there in the canopy," pointing at the tops of the tall trees which bordered the lane. Ten minutes ago, I mused. We couldn't be too late already, could we? As we stood, craning our necks and scanning, some of us were trampling the vegetation on the edge of the lane. Suddenly a resident islander, an irate woman, came on the scene and demanded who we were and who was in charge. She called us a bunch of hooligans with no respect for the countryside.

"Sssssh! You'll scare the bird away", said a desperate birder in a loud whisper. It was a very sad and embarrassing occasion, and I'm glad to say that this sort of thing happens only rarely these days in the Scillies. I felt considerable sympathy with her. It must have been disconcerting to say the least to find a hundred and fifty great hairy birders, most of them bearded and looking as though they had slept under a hedge (and some of them probably had) outside your peaceful island cottage. Certainly in the past, the rougher and some of the more over-enthusiastic birders had caused undeniable offence to the islanders, but nowadays a happy compromise has been found. The birders have had to learn to behave themselves while the islanders have a very welcome extension to their holiday season.

Seconds later the woman's audience evaporated in front of her. As so often happens on Scilly, there was a stampede. This stampede was to the other end of Watermill Lane. The Olivaceous Warbler had found what it wanted in a garden at the far end of the lane. The crowd squeezed itself into the limited space available and waited. Moments later, a delightful little grey bird was doing acrobatics in the bushes in front of us. It was oblivious of its audience and ignored the "Oooh's" and "Aaaah's" from its admiring fans. It was very fond of hoverflies and adept at catching them. It was larger than the average warbler and had a domed head with an almost flat forehead. Its beak was very un-warbler like, large and looking as though it had been borrowed from a flycatcher. John trained his telescope on it, and many of us around him had excellent views. I was even able to see the scales on its claws. As we enjoyed the bird, people were arriving all the time, and the crush in the limited space was getting less and less pleasant. It was time to go. We were just leaving as Clive arrived; we heard later that he saw it well.

We were in no hurry because the next boat to Tresco wasn't

until a quarter past two. We walked slowly back towards the town, deriving considerable pleasure from seeing breathless Olivaceous-bound birders who asked anxiously, "Is the Olivaceous still there? Have you seen it?"

We would reply casually and with an air of slight superiority, "Well it was five, ten, twenty minutes ago", depending on how far we had walked back.

Is this the best way to get a better view?

The town was completely deserted when we arrived back. Everyone it seemed was hell bent towards Watermill Lane or still on Tresco. By now, it must have been getting quite unpleasant up there, especially as the viewing area was so restricted. There were a hundred and fifty people, at least when I saw it, and that was more than the lane could accommodate comfortably. There were now an estimated eight hundred birders on the islands. By the time they all arrived there, it would be awful; luckily it seemed the bird wasn't particularly bothered by people.

We had a leisurely pie and a pint for lunch in the Mermaid. While eating, we watched boatload after boatload of birders returning from Tresco, much as the Giant and I had watched returning from Bryher having tried for the Yellowthroat. Excellent, I thought. Everything was going precisely as I had planned. At two fifteen we joined half a boatload of birders who were Dusky Warbler bound.

When we arrived on Tresco we made our way back to the maize field. To my surprise, there was still quite a crowd there. They had the right idea though, I reckon. Their goal for the day was the Dusky Warbler, and no Olivaceous Warbler was going to tempt them away. As the Giant would put it, "One tick at a time, that's all I asked sweet Jesus, one tick at a time." Not a bad motto when you think about it.

Now that the habits of the Dusky Warbler were better known, it seemed that the best chances of seeing it were from the gate where I had glimpsed it the previous day. Birders had made an arrangement with the owner whereby groups of thirty could have a go by the gate for half an hour at a time. It was a bit like the Swainson's Thrush in the Parsonage. A young girl birder was trying to organise it. I felt rather sorry for her because one or two birders became rather abusive. They didn't approve of the scheme and accused her of not allowing them enough time when their allotted span had come to an end unsuccessfully. When you consider that these voluntary wardens give up good birding time to supervise birders on a private site, people should be more grateful to them. If there were no one who was prepared to do this, nine times out of ten the owner would refuse to let the birders in to see the bird at all. We joined a queue, and it wasn't that long before it was our turn to have a go. We had our half hour by the gate, but during that time nothing happened. Luckily for us, it appeared that the Olivaceous Warbler was continuing to be a magnet, and there were now so few people there that it was soon our turn again. We hadn't been by the gate very long when there was a mass exodus to a nearby hillside.

The Dusky Warbler had been re-located. About fifty telescopes were trained from the crowd seated on the hillside onto a hedgerow below us.

"Are you on it?" I asked a nearby birder as I joined them.

"Yes", he replied and gave me directions. A little grey bird was moving busily along the base of the hedge. With my binoculars it was quite impossible to distinguish it from any other species of warbler at that range. All the time the warbler was slowly making its way along the hedge away from us. If it carried on in that direction it wouldn't be that long before it passed in front of the gateway we had just left.

"It's going back towards the hedge by the gate", I whispered to John who was sitting next to me. "Come on, let's go", I whispered urgently. "We're getting lousy views here. Be as casual as possible, or everyone will want to follow us."

With a total lack of apparent urgency, we stood up slowly and made our way back down to the field with the gate.

"Can we go back in?" I asked the girl who was still wardening the field, which was now deserted.

"I guess so", she answered with an air of resignation. "I give up!" It must have been very difficult for her. Moments ago everyone was desperate to be in that field, but now we had it to ourselves. If we had played our cards right, the bird should arrive in front of the gateway at any moment.

As we couldn't see very far along the hedgerow to the left we could have absolutely no idea what the bird was up to. For all we knew, it might have changed its mind and be moving back up the hill. Very few, perhaps another four birders, came to join us. We waited and waited. Where was the bird? Surely I hadn't got it wrong? I was still convinced it was coming in our direction. In any case, the hedge by the gate was its regular beat, so it ought to pass by us sooner or later.

After waiting nearly half an hour, the unmistakable tack…tack…tack of the Dusky Warbler could be heard to our left. It was coming from the direction of the crowd on the hill! I felt rather chuffed and at the same time excited at the prospect of seeing this bird really well.

"We must be as quiet as we know how", I whispered. "Hear that tacking noise? That's the Dusky Warbler and it's coming this way." We froze. Seconds later a greyish brown Chiffchaff-like bird came into view. It started bobbing about just feet in front of us and was completely unconcerned. It was less than ten feet away, and the half dozen of us had it all to ourselves. Its most noticeable feature was the very marked supercilium and eye stripe, but apart from that it was a very smart little bird now we could see it properly. For the next few minutes we hardly dared breathe. While everyone else was up there on the hillside, we enjoyed really privileged views of this very timid bird.

My plans had worked out marvellously, and the predictions had been spot on. I had definitely made the right decision not to dash off to Tresco on the early boat and, as a result, had been in the right place for the bird of the day, the Olivaceous Warbler. Now I had enjoyed fantastic views of one of the most difficult birds on Scilly! Perhaps this sort of planning is what Scilly birding is all about, but it would always be a gamble, and that was part of the fun. Perhaps I had just been very lucky;

anyway, I felt pretty good.

What do they say about pride coming before a fall? I was about to fall!

Since I had enjoyed the bird of the moment, I decided to leave for St. Mary's. I arrived at the quay to find a boat three quarters full. I climbed aboard to wait for the boat to fill up. Someone on the boat noticed a small crowd of birders just along the coast obviously onto something.

"What do you reckon they've got?" I asked my neighbour on the boat.

"I believe there's a Tawny Pipit round there", someone suggested.

"That's alright then", I replied. "I saw the one the other day on the airport." We continued to wait for the boat to fill up, which it was doing remarkably slowly. Half an hour later, a birder climbed aboard and announced cheerfully.

"There's a really fabulous Bluethroat two hundred yards back along the track. I've just come from watching it really close. It's just hopping about amongst the bracken." Although Bluethroats are reckoned to be amongst the commoner rarities on Scilly, it was astonishing how many people had never caught up with one, and I was one of them. They are skulking birds, and once they have been lost they are almost impossible to relocate. I was very anxious to see this bird and so broke an important Scilly rule. I jumped ship! There are two good reasons why this was irresponsible. First, the boatmen always count the number of people they take to the other islands. They also count them when they get back on board. In this way no one gets left behind overnight. My leaving like that would confuse the figures. Secondly it was past four thirty and the boatman was anxious to leave.

"I'll be back in five minutes", I shouted over my shoulder as

I shot off up the road. As I ran I met amused birders coming the other way.

"Is it still there?" I gasped desperately.

"Yes, it's back there on the right...in the bracken. Only another two hundred yards or so...fantastic bird." This bird was supposed to have a really well-marked necklace with a few blue feathers above it. A male Bluethroat in the spring must be one of the most stunning birds with its bright, royal blue throat. In autumn, this lovely blue is lost. The best one can hope for is a black necklace below a clean white throat with a trace of blue on the necklace. Most birds are juvenile and look streaky like juvenile robins. I ran as best I could but was hindered by my paratrooper's boots, my jacket and two thick pullovers. About eighty yards short of the site I bumped into John.

"Have you seen it?" I spluttered.

"I was one of the ones who found it", he replied, and I felt thoroughly gripped. If I had not dashed off from the Dusky Warbler so impatiently I would have been with him. As it was, I had just spent a boring three-quarters of an hour sitting in a boat. Evidently he and about five others had been strolling back when the Bluethroat hopped out in front of them.

"Come on John", I cajoled. "Come and show me where it is."

"Okay", he replied. "It shouldn't be too difficult, but we'd better hurry. The boat's going to leave at any minute."

"It won't leave without us", I said, trying to reassure myself as much as him. "There are still a lot of blokes ambling back along the road." We hadn't gone more than a few yards when a couple of blokes rounded the corner in front of us.

"Is the Bluethroat still there?" I asked desperately.

"It was half a minute ago when we left it", they replied. "We left because it hopped off out of view into the bracken.

There's no one there any more, so you're going to have one hell of a job if you want to see it." Desperately, John and I went and had a quick look, but it was no good. We couldn't hang about, because most of those on the road would be down at the boat by now. I felt badly gripped, especially after I thought I'd been such a very good Scilly birder all day. Still it wasn't quite dark yet. Something might have turned up on St. Mary's.

We got back to the boat, and I had to suffer the embarrassment of an angry tongue lashing by the boatman in front of two hundred other birders. When we reached the quay the town was strangely deserted. I quickened my pace and walked round to the Porthcressa. There on the board, scrawled in yellow chalk at least a foot high were the words:

PANIC! 17.10   Rock Thrush   Peninnis

It was now five thirty. I had seen plenty of Rock Thrushes abroad, so this would only be another UK tick for me. At that moment I had no idea just how important this particular UK tick would be. I glanced at the rest of the information on the board and noticed that a Richard's Pipit, still a potential lifer for me, had turned up on Telegraph Hill, and...oh my God! There was a Bluethroat on Porth Hellick Pool! This last item raised my spirits considerably. I decided to go and try for the Richard's Pipit, even though this Rock Thrush was an apparent panic bird.

I was on the outskirts of town when I bumped into a loan birder huffing and puffing in the direction of Peninnis Head.

"Any news on the Richard's?" I asked.

"Have you seen the Rock Thrush?" he demanded breathlessly.

"No", I replied.

"Bloody hell, there's only a ruddy Rock Thrush up on Peninnis Head, and you're worried about a Richard's? I haven't a clue, mate…sorry."

"But a Richard's is a lifer", I objected as he walked briskly away in the opposite direction. A Rock Thrush would only be a UK tick.

"Same here", he shouted. "But it's one hell of a UK tick!" He quickly vanished. Evidently this Rock Thrush really was causing a stir: a real panic bird. The light was fading, so perhaps I really ought to see the Rock Thrush and try for the Richard's Pipit afterwards, providing it wasn't too dark.

The path up to Peninnis Head was crowded with birders rushing in all directions. On top of the hill and silhouetted against the skyline, the effect of the massed ranks of birders was like an army before the start of an epic mediaeval battle. Every birder in the islands had congregated to see this Rock Thrush. First reports suggested that it was still there but being very difficult to see.

Shortly after I arrived in approximately the right place, there was an excited murmur. Someone was onto the bird. I heard muffled mutterings about bramble and a dry stone wall. I looked at the area in question but in the gathering gloom could see nothing.

"It's dived", a young man exclaimed close by. While it was visible, birders without a telescope had been queuing for a glimpse through someone else's. Several lucky birders had managed to see it, but I wasn't one of them.

"It's up again", came an urgent whisper from close by. Seconds later it was my turn to have a glimpse through the telescope and it was still there. I saw an indistinct bluish grey-backed thrush with a red breast. It may have had a reddish tail, but I couldn't tell in that light. The image in the telescope was hazy and distant, and the bird was half turned away. After I had had my turn, I waited for a few moments to see if the bird would take it into its head to fly over in our direction. It didn't, so I decided to rush to Telegraph Hill and see if I could see the Richard's Pipit. On the way, I passed a perplexed Leon and Bob coming up the hill still Rock Thrush-bound.

"What the hell are you going that way for?" a perplexed Leon demanded. "The Rock Thrush is this way."

"Richard's Pipit...Telegraph Hill", I gasped.

"Good Lord!" he exclaimed. "There's only a bloody Rock Thrush up here, that's all." A look of incredulous amazement spread over his face. It seemed as though this Rock Thrush was going to rival even the Yellowthroat for the title of bird of the year. I dashed on towards Telegraph Hill. The light was fading fast. Could I make it to Telegraph Hill before it was impossible to see anything? I began to doubt it. I was almost relieved when I bumped into a chap coming the other way.

"Any news on the Richard's?" I puffed.

"Hasn't been seen for an hour and a half", he replied. "It flew off over the fields. Anyway, what's all this I hear about a Rock Thrush?" I told him, and he was gone in a flash. I sauntered back to town and the Porthcressa where I bumped into Chris and Tessa.

"Seen the Rock Thrush?" I enquired breezily.

"No, I bloody haven't!" Chris replied irritably. The latest news on the Rock Thrush began to filter through on Radio Birdbrain. Evidently it was showing well on a lawn near the hospital. By now it was almost completely dark. Was it really worth legging it all the way back up there? Scarcely, I thought. Even though I had had a glimpse of the bird, it would be rather nice to see it pulling worms out of a lawn. Even though the hospital was at the Hugh Town end of Peninnis, time was of the essence. The first stars were beginning to twinkle overhead.

When we arrived at the spot, it was a lot further out of town than we had been led to believe. It was nowhere near the hospital nor was there a lawn to be seen, and the Rock Thrush wasn't pecking peacefully anywhere nearby. The site was in fact a typical Scilly-ploughed field with lots of ruts and weeds. A thrush-sized bird hopped up onto a wall on the far side of the field. With my binoculars I couldn't even see it; it was so dark. Eventually with great difficulty, I was given directions onto the bird. It might have been a Rock Thrush, but on the other hand it was just as likely it was a Blackbird, a Starling or a Wheatear. In any case, it was quite hopeless, so we returned to town.

Personally I had had very little difficulty getting my glimpse of the Rock Thrush. I hadn't enjoyed crippling views, but there was no doubt that the bird I had seen was the bird in question. I was utterly astonished when I heard later in the Mermaid that none of the others had seen it at all. In fact, it turned out that very few of the eight hundred birders who had tried for it had seen it.

"What did you see?" they demanded. I described what I had seen of the bird.

"Why wasn't it a Yankee Robin, then?" they asked scathingly. "You're surely not going to tick it on that sighting, are you?" I was given the third degree. It was all very difficult. In any case, I really wasn't that concerned about ticking a Rock Thrush as I had seen several in both Spain and Greece. However, since so few had seen it, ticking this bird became very important indeed. Everyone with me had said it was the Rock Thrush, and I had seen it and agreed with them. Even so, I suppose I had to admit that the views I had had were scarcely sufficient to distinguish it from several of the other scarce thrushes. It was a difficult dilemma, but I stood my ground. I still reckoned I had seen the bird everyone else was after. I determined it was on my list as a UK tick.

Later I found out just why this Rock Thrush was so important to everyone. There had not been a genuinely tickable one in Britain for many years. There had been one comparatively recently in Kent, and a large number of people had gone to see it. But it was now thought to be what birders refer to scathingly as a wire hopper! That is, a bird which has escaped from captivity. Until this Scilly Rock Thrush had arrived, there had been pencilled Rock Thrush ticks in rather a lot of notebooks. Everyone was now very keen to rub out the pencil and replace it with indelible ink.

In Scilly that evening, the log at the Porthcressa indicated a very rosy picture indeed. The good birds were attracting mainland birders in droves, and the helicopter was fully booked. I heard it was even hard to get a place on the *Scillonian*. Good birds reported that evening were as follows:

Rock Thrush	*1 Penninis*
Olivaceous Warbler	*1 Watermill Lane*
Bluethroat	*1 Tresco*
Bluethroat	*1 Porth Hellick Lake*
Dusky Warbler	*1 Tresco*
Blackpoll Warbler	*1 St. Agnes*
Ortolan Bunting	*3 Rocky Hills*
Ortolan Bunting	*1 Tresco*
Tawny Pipit	*1 Tresco*
Red-breasted Flycatcher	2 (total for the day but no mention of where they had been seen)
Common Rosefinch	*1 Longstones*
Common Rosefinch	*1 Salakee Farm*

Corncrake	*1 Longstones*
Little Bunting	*1 Rocky Hills*
Rustic Bunting	*2 Tresco*
Richard's Pipit	*1 Telegraph Hill*

I knew exactly what I was going to do, and it says something for my personal confidence in my Rock Thrush tick. I was going to see one of those Bluethroats, come what may.

14. The day of the long wait... followed by a dip

Although I had intended to be down at Porth Hellick at first light, I didn't manage to get there until eight o'clock. A handful of birders were there when I arrived. Evidently I was not the only one keen to see this Bluethroat. About half an hour before I had arrived, the bird had been seen on a small cleared area close to the path, so at least it was still there. At the Log the previous evening, when the Bluethroat had been called for Porth Hellick, Mike Rogers had said:

"Those of you who saw the Bluethroat owe me a drink. It was me who cleared that area for you." Five minutes later amidst cheers, a birder went up to Mike Rogers at the microphone with a double whisky!

This morning it was very quiet and still in front of Mike Rogers' clearing. The birders there were waiting in absolute silence; one did not even dare to cough. Any new arrivals were quickly brow beaten into the same total silence. In spite of these precautions, there was no sign of the Bluethroat. A Firecrest appeared in a pine above our heads and a Water Rail padded out bravely into the middle of the clearing; it was only two or three yards in front of us. Suddenly it appeared to notice how close the birders were for the first time. It looked startled and embarrassed, and dashed into the reeds like a bolt of lightning. I had never seen a Water Rail move so fast. Normally they walk so sedately and with great decorum.

Another bird, which appeared and caused a minor stir, was a Reed Bunting. This was admittedly the first I had seen on the trip. Later when I told the others about it they scarcely believed me; they are a rarity in Scilly. It seemed strange to be taking Rustic, Little and Ortolan Buntings in our stride, while Reed Buntings were considered exciting. The only other highlight of the morning was a Common Redstart. Having a red tail, it caused a momentary excitement, as Bluethroats also have a red tail. At midday, after a four-hour vigil in total silence, I made the decision to leave in fifteen minutes. I'd go back into town for lunch via Telegraph Hill just in case the Richard's Pipit had appeared. Nothing happened during those fifteen minutes, so I set off for Telegraph Hill.

When I got there, the news was predictably depressing. The bird hadn't been seen all day. I walked down to the Porthcressa for lunch. Maybe the rather stunning Bluethroat I had dipped on yesterday was giving crippling views on Tresco. If this were the case, I would simply have to become an island hopper again. I got a nasty shock when I arrived at the Porthcressa. Emblazoned across the board was written:

Bluethroat   Porth Hellick 12.20 – showing well

This was utterly ridiculous and grossly unfair. I had chosen to leave Porth Hellick, after a four-hour-long vigil, minutes... perhaps even seconds before the Bluethroat had appeared. The air went blue!

Feeling very annoyed, I went into the Porthcressa for a coffee and a hot pie. In there I heard all about what was happening to the Rock Thrush. The poor wretched bird was being chased from Peninnis Head to Porth Hellick Cove by an increasing army of birders. The crowd had started to assemble before dawn had even broken and was now truly enormous. At dawn, it was glimpsed by a few, only to be pushed to the next headland by the increasing number of impatient and desperate birders. I was becoming more and more grateful that I had seen it, even if I had only had a brief glimpse. At that moment I was frankly ashamed of my fellow birders. Why couldn't they just sit down and wait patiently like we'd been doing all morning for the Bluethroat... behave like real naturalists for once? Perhaps then the bird might come to them.

After I had finished my lunch I stood up reluctantly and set off with the prospect of another endless vigil ahead. As I walked out of town I heard that a rather well-marked Common Rosefinch was showing well between Salakee Farm and the airport. I decided to go and have a look at that first. Common Rosefinches, normally one of the 'commoner rarities' on Scilly, had been distinctly scarce in 1984, so it wasn't that surprising that it had attracted quite a crowd. I approached the group.

"Is it showing?" I enquired delicately.

"It was a few moments ago", one of the birders replied. "It's down in that thick undergrowth at the moment, but it should be up again in a minute or two. It wasn't long before it reappeared to feed on the seeds of a taller plant than most in the field. It was indeed a particularly smart Rosefinch, and I enjoyed excellent views of it through a friendly birder's telescope. I was astonished at the size of the beak, a real nutcracker. Its plumage was a subtle cream to buff, and the white wing bars were really quite well defined. After I had enjoyed a really good look, it flew off to another part of the field and disappeared, at least temporarily. Very often Rosefinches fly in flocks of Linnets and Goldfinches, but this bird was keeping to itself. I left to return to my vigil at Porth Hellick Pool. On the way there, I bumped into birder after birder who assured me the Bluethroat was still showing well.

I was two hundred yards from Porth Hellick Pool when I met again the three serious birders from Christchurch.

"Hello Simon", they greeted me cheerfully. "The Bluethroat's showing really nicely at the moment, though it has been wandering around towards the other side of the Pool. We've just been enjoying really excellent views. As we left, it had just popped into a reed bed, but I expect it will re-emerge before long."

"That's great news. Thanks", I enthused as I left them and walked away as nonchalantly as my desperation would allow.

"I bet he runs as soon as he gets out of view", I heard one of them say in an overloud whisper as I left them. As soon as I was out of view, and I hoped earshot, I did just that. When I saw them later, they remarked derisively.

"We heard you running. We heard your heavy boots pounding down that path after the Bluethroat. Talk about a desperate twitcher!" They were quite right, of course, but I often wonder whether they actually heard me running or just knew that I would.

I arrived at the smaller, more rickety of the two Porth Hellick hides.

"Any news?" I asked tentatively as I found a space.

"Well yes", someone replied. "It was running along the mud in front of those reeds a few moments ago, and it ought to be out in a minute or two. It's been diving in and out of the reeds pretty regularly for the past three quarters of an hour or so."

"Fantastic", I exclaimed and started to wait with renewed enthusiasm. Five minutes passed followed by ten…then twenty.

"That's funny", mused my informant. "It ought to have come out by now. Where could it have gone? It seemed to be coming towards us from the right. Perhaps it decided to go round the corner after all and out of sight."

"No doubt!" I replied irritably. "I'm beginning to think this

Bluethroat's got something personal against me. Apart from a break for lunch, I've been here solidly since eight o'clock this morning."

"Good grief!" exclaimed my informant. "Yes, that is bad luck." If it really were coming in our direction, it would be obscured by a clump of reeds immediately in front of us. I glanced up at the main hide, and there were a few people in it. Perhaps that was the place to be. Just then a bird, a water vole or something scuttled across a tiny gap immediately in front of us. If it had been the Bluethroat, and I had no evidence to suggest that it was except that it had been coming in our direction, I was wasting my time staying where I was. I dithered for a moment or two, trying to decide on the best course of action, then went off to the main hide. When I arrived, there was just a young family present.

"Have you seen it?" I asked.

"What?" they asked in return.

"The Bluethroat", I replied.

"Oh! Is there a Bluethroat", they asked in surprise. "That's nice. What do they look like?" It wasn't going to be found by the others in this hide, that was obvious. I stared out of the hide, intently trying to take in as much of the shore as I could. A few moments later the family left, so I had the hide to myself. My eyes darted nervously from the spot where the Bluethroat had been seen to the birders in the other hide. I tried to make out whether or not they were looking at it. My eyes then darted to the point where I predicted it ought to emerge if I had been right, and the thing, which had darted across that little gap, was indeed it. I spent twenty lonely minutes up there in that hide in a very jumpy state. This is ridiculous, I thought to myself. I'm never going to see it up here on my own.

Suddenly I noticed that the birders in the other hide had

concentrated their attentions on a particular piece of lake shore. I stared intently at the spot they appeared to be looking at, but could see nothing. There was obviously only one thing for it and that was to go back to the other hide.

"Seen it recently?" I asked as I returned to the space I had abandoned about a half an hour previously.

"You really shouldn't have gone off to that other hide", they replied. "It's been coming out off and on ever since you left. It came out of the reeds over there just a few moments ago, but it's gone back in for the moment. It should be out again before too long."

"I doubt it", I groaned. "Now that I've come back it's probably gone for good."

"There it is…it's out again", one of them whispered.

"Where?" I asked urgently. I was given excellent directions but it was no use. I simply couldn't see it.

"I've got it in the scope now", said another chap. "Here, have a look…oh dear, it's gone back in." This fiasco was fast turning into a farce. This time it was an uncomfortable five minutes before someone reported that it was out yet again. Once more I followed the instructions carefully, and this time, at long last, I could see a little grey coloured bird padding along the shore. It behaved more like a wader than a passerine. I watched it for perhaps a minute before it dashed into the reeds and out of sight.

Finally, I had seen a Bluethroat! It almost felt like an anticlimax after all the effort. This one was not a spectacular bird by any stretch of the imagination, but it was at least tickable. It was only a brief moment before it re-appeared. It darted out of the reeds…stood motionless for a moment or two then dashed on for a few feet before stopping again. It was moving closer to us, and the views I was getting were improving all the time. It had a flecked throat with the traces of a necklace dividing the flecked area from the paler colour of its belly. The flecking, using considerable imagination, perhaps did look bluish and the red patches on the tail were much more evident as it moved closer. These were becoming much better views, and at last I could relax. Already I had been thinking of Bluethroat as my bogey bird, even though it was less than twenty-four hours since I had first dipped on Tresco. Later I heard reports of another birder who had found the Bluethroat difficult to get to grips with.

"Where's this Bluethroat?" he demanded aggressively as he had entered the Porth Hellick hide.

"It's on the far side of the lake...over there, just below that large clump of reeds."

"Where! I can't f*****g see it, where the s**t is it?"

"It's still over there", said the other chap patiently. "Just where I told you it was."

"Where? Well I can't f*****g see it. Where the f***'s it?" The patient birder sighed and gave him the instructions all over again.

"It's bloody not!" shouted the desperate birder. "I still can't f*****g well see the f*****g thing", he ranted.

"It's just gone", said the patient birder. "At least it has as far as you're concerned." I suppose we all get pretty desperate from time to time about birds, but I hope he now realises that that sort of desperation is strictly against all the unwritten rules of Scilly birding.

Having seen the Bluethroat, I left Porth Hellick. There was still the unbelievably elusive Richard's Pipit somewhere on Telegraph Hill. I made my way through Higher Moors towards Longstones. Here was another small group of birders looking for yet another Common Rosefinch. I had brief, but distant, views of the Short-toed Lark and then went into the Centre for a coffee. Here I heard the news that the Richard's Pipit hadn't been seen all day. For the time being at least, it began to look as though I had run out of good birds to go for.

There was a small butterfly farm at the Longstones Centre, which was quite a pleasant attraction. It was free, so before I had my coffee I decided to go in and have a look. It comprised a large greenhouse filled with tropical plants, with the atmosphere inside heady with the perfume of the tropics. It was sticky and humid. There were large tropical swallowtail butterflies with wings opening and closing slowly as they probed flowers for nectar. On the ceiling an enormous Owl butterfly from South America displayed large, owl-like eyes on its hind wings. It sat motionless, and it was hard to believe it was still alive. Three Painted Ladies sat huddled together in a corner, a migrant butterfly, which was scarce in 1984. These were just a few of the butterflies I noticed. One butterfly present in there in some numbers was the Milkweed or Monarch. This is a species which, like the Yellowthroat or Swainson's Thrush, finds its way across the Atlantic from America occasionally. In fact, there are now thriving colonies, which have become established this side of the Atlantic in the Canary Islands. The chance of these transatlantic butterflies occurring in the Scilly Isles is far greater than anywhere else in Britain. It would be very sad if shadows of doubt were now to be cast on all future Scilly Milkweed butterflies because there was a chance they might have escaped from this butterfly farm.

I was about to leave to go and have my coffee when Leon and Bob came in to join me. Bob and I had had many evening chats about butterflies in the Mermaid, so he knew of my interest.

"Show us around then, Simon", suggested Bob. We had a

leisurely look round then returned into the café part for our coffee.

"Leon's feeling chuffed today", Bob announced.

"Why's that?" I asked.

"He's caught up half a tick on me", Bob replied. The half tick was the Rock Thrush, which Leon, like so many others, had seen in Kent. Bob was one of the very few who had seen another, less controversial one. There was a happy, slightly self-satisfied and relaxed atmosphere in the air as we sipped our coffee together. There was nothing that any of us had not seen now, even though there were an excellent number of really good birds about.

"In birding", Leon began, relaxing back in his chair, "and especially Scilly birding, the important thing is never to let yourself get behind. The Bluethroat is today's bird, but the Olivaceous Warbler, Rock Thrush and Dusky Warbler were all yesterday's birds. Simon, whatever you do, you must never ever allow yourself to become a yesterday's man. If you do, you'll find yourself dithering around, wondering whether to go for yesterday's, today's or even the day before yesterday's birds. If you can possibly avoid it, never go to bed with a yesterday's bird still to see."

It was a good feeling. Here I was relaxing and talking on equal terms with two of the most experienced birders on Scilly. Being a today's man, I had had twenty-six ticks during the trip so far. This was a total that most of my companions thought positively disgusting!

After relaxing over our coffee and chatting together casually, we decided we might as well go and see if we could get better views of the Rock Thrush. It really didn't matter if we saw it or not though, because we were all today's men. We had already seen it. We wandered off through Higher Moors, past

Porth Hellick and a small crowd of birders who still hadn't seen the Bluethroat. Now that I had it safely under my belt, it was hard to believe that there were still people who hadn't. We walked up to a cluster of rocks close to the airport known as Giant's Castle. Coming the other way, and struggling against a stiffening breeze, were Chris and Tessa. They had serious and slightly pained expressions on their faces; in fact, they didn't look happy at all. They hadn't got to grips with the Rock Thrush yet...nor the Bluethroat, and both were ticks. At that moment they were torn between the attractions of both.

"A typical example of yesterday's men", Leon scoffed. Chris and Tessa's fortunes were about to change dramatically.

"There's the Rock Thrush!" I was astonished as I noticed this stunningly beautiful bird perched on a rock no more than ten yards in front of us. Its demeanour was that of a Wheatear. Once we had settled ourselves down with as little commotion as possible, I glanced over my shoulder. I was pleased and relieved to see that Chris and Tessa had also spotted it and had a telescope trained on it.

We could now study this delightful bird at leisure. It had a greyish blue back with white edging to the primaries. It had a lovely chestnut red breast and a tail the colour of a Redstart's which it bobbed constantly. In fact, it did look very like an oversized Redstart. It flitted happily from rock to rock no doubt relieved to have lost, at least temporarily, the hoard of birders who were pursuing it. As we watched, it moved slowly towards Porth Hellick and the headlands beyond. It wasn't many minutes before the first birder was silhouetted against the skyline above Giant's Castle. It wasn't that long before desperate birders were all around us like fox hounds that have run a fox to earth.

"Did you see it?" one of them demanded impatiently.

"What might I have seen?" Leon answered enigmatically, being deliberately obtuse.

"The Rock Thrush, of course", spluttered the birder. He looked at the five of us as though we were all terminally thick.

"Oh that!" Leon replied dismissively. "Haven't you lot managed to catch up with it yet."

"No, we bloody haven't. Come on, did you see it or not?"

"Until you lot arrived it was sitting peacefully on that rock over there, not ten yards away. We've just been having utterly stonking views."

"Where's it gone now?"

"Out beyond Porth Hellick and those headlands in the distance, I should think", he replied. "If only you were to sit down patiently, it might even come to you", Leon added sarcastically, knowing the chances of that happening were minimal. As we talked, more and more exhausted birders poured over the skyline. This mighty hoard had been pursuing the Rock Thrush from Peninnis Head to Giant's Castle and beyond since first light. Someone observed that they hadn't seen it eating anything. That was hardly surprising, the pursuing birders were scarcely giving it a chance. However, perhaps the bird was having a laugh at the birders' expense after all. As we had just observed, it only takes a few minutes for a bird to put a considerable distance between itself and its would-be admirers. With a bit of luck, the Rock Thrush would only consider the birding army as a very mild irritation. Having flown from Southern Europe, it would be a minor problem for it to fly the short distance to the Cornish mainland where it would probably be lost forever. Leon began to chuckle as he recognised the elite of the birding world huffing and puffing past us only to dip yet again when they arrived up at Giant's Rocks.

"Yesterday's men, the lot of them!" Leon scoffed with

amused scorn. There was little else for us, who were today's men, to do except wait for the Mermaid to open. We did see a smart male Black Redstart on rubbish near the island's incinerator, but that was all. It was getting dark, and a savage wind was increasing in strength all the time, a wind which could bring in lots more good birds. I only had one more day's birding left, so I probably wouldn't see them.

Sea watching can be most rewarding when conditions are right and the wind is strong. I had never been on one of those historic Cornish sea watches when Sabine's Gulls, Leach's Petrels and Pomarine Skuas fly past at the rate of several an hour, but I had heard all about them. The wind was blowing fiercely, so perhaps tomorrow I would be lucky.

15. My last day in the Scilly Isles... during 1984 at least

When I woke up next morning the wind was still howling and whining outside. The chances of any bird, or other living thing come to that, showing itself above the shelter of cover seemed distinctly remote. That is, apart from the odd Scilly birder of course. I got up and had a hearty breakfast before setting off towards Peninnis Head to do a sea watch. In the Mermaid the night before we had discussed sea watching. Although it may be obvious to most, it hadn't been to me that the best place to sea watch is on a headland where the wind is blowing parallel to the coast. A seabird being driven towards the coast will alter course to avoid it, while a bird finding land to the left or right will be quite happy flying parallel to it. People do sea watch in the Scillies, but the general opinion is that it is never very spectacular.

As I walked down from the Garrison I noted the wind direction which, though very strong still, had moderated a little. Perhaps Giant's Castle would be a better bet, I thought to myself. I decided to delay my decision until I had been to the Porthcressa for the latest news. There was the inevitable Rock Thrush news on the board but otherwise nothing new. When I had walked around Porthcressa Bay I was in a better position to assess the wind direction and made the decision to go on to Giant's Castle. When I arrived, there were still one or two Rock Thrush botherers waiting to see which way to dash next. These were real yesterday's men! Luckily for the Rock Thrush, there were very few of them left, but I found I had a distinct antagonism towards them. Perhaps if I hadn't managed to see the Rock Thrush, I might have had a kindlier attitude towards them. All I wanted to do was to find a sheltered spot where I could settle down out of the wind and pick out Pomarine Skuas, Leach's Petrels and Sabine's Gulls.

There were already one or two other sea watchers, and I joined them. I spent two hours in all. The waves out to sea were enormous, looking like great sculptures in jade. Each was decorated with a plume of white foam. They crashed into the rocks below us with a crump sending spray fifty feet into the air towards us. In spite of this, sea watching is a more peaceful way to bird watch; far less frenetic than chasing after some newly arrived migrant. Briefly I tried to string a juvenile Kittiwake into a Sabine's Gull; anyone who has never tried to do that is deceiving themselves! The only other birds to pass were a large number of Gannets, Kittiwakes and a variety of gulls.

After I had been sea watching for a couple of hours, I noticed that the birds passing the headlands seemed to be going just that much closer to the next headland north beyond Porth Hellick Bay. I told the others of my conclusions, and they said that the headland in question was called Deep Point. I wished the others good luck and set off in that direction. I didn't even get as far as Porth Hellick before I bumped into a birder.

"There's a stink up on the Garrison."

"What on earth do you mean?" I asked bemused.

"A Pink Stink!" he replied, looking at me as though I were stupid.

"What the devil's a Pink Stink?" I was utterly confused. I had visions of a major industrial disaster with pink fumes drifting off in all direction, or perhaps he was referring to some disastrous problem with the island's sewerage system.

"Don't you know what a Pink Stink is?" He clearly regarded me as of very low intelligence.

"No", I replied. "No, I don't."

"It's a juv. Rose-coloured Starling of course", he informed me. Mature Rose-coloured Starlings with their contrasting plumages of pink and black are very attractive. The juvenile birds, which arrive in the Scilly Islands in late autumn, have a rather washed-out, pink plumage. Hence their rather derisory nick name.

"That's great. Is it a nice adult one?" I asked naively.

"I don't know, but I doubt it", he replied. "They never are." Rose-coloured Starlings are another of the commoner Scilly rarities and usually at least an annual event. I abandoned my pilgrimage to Deep Point and walked briskly back toward the town. I passed a small group of Common Rosefinch watchers close to Salakee Farm.

"Heard about this Rosy Starling?" I asked as I hurried past.

"No, where?"

"Somewhere up on the Garrison. At least that's what I was told." I puffed and hurried on. It was annoying to be pulled back from the centre of the island, but I was prepared to do so for a Rose-coloured Starling would be yet another tick and definitely a today's bird. I could also find out if there was anything new from the Porthcressa board; surely this wind ought to bring in something. As I approached the outskirts of town I noticed there were very few birders about. Soon I was able to ask a couple of birders leaving the town about the Rose-coloured Starling.

"It's not been seen since eleven o'clock", they informed me. "It flew over the Garrison in the direction of the incinerator, I believe. There are still a few birders left up on the Garrison, but no one's seen it recently. I doubt if it's there for a moment."

When I arrived at the Porthcressa I heard the full story. Someone staying in the campsite on the Garrison had poked his head out of his tent and had seen it. It had promptly flown off and was never seen again. The board at the Porthcressa was equally depressing. At the top, it announced:

Penninis   Sea watching – unspectacular

...and I had seen all the other birds that were mentioned. I had lunch and then walked back to Porth Hellick and beyond to Deep Point for another sea watch.

I was joined by another chap. We decided to give it another two hours. Unfortunately the wind had abated slightly, but the passing waves were still of a prodigious size. They looked just right to hold a flock of shearwaters or the odd skua. However, we saw nothing more exciting than Gannets and Kittiwakes. After two hours I glanced over my shoulder. There behind us, about to deposit on us like a bathroom shower, was the blackest, most evil looking cloud imaginable. We dashed off to the Porth Hellick hide for shelter but found a small hut beforehand which was lucky. The storm broke long before we made Porth Hellick. The hut gave us some protection, but we still got soaked to the skin.

Once the storm had abated, the sun came out strongly, and we dried out fairly quickly. The main question was what to do next. I hadn't heard the Olivaceous Warbler's call yet, so went up to Watermill Lane to pay my respects once more. Now that the Yellowthroat and Swainson's Thrush had been seen by many, and the Rock Thrush chased by most, the title of bird of the moment had reverted to the Olivaceous Warbler. This bird must have been the most obliging crippler of 1984. It had become even more of an exhibitionist since I had seen it last. It was diving in and out of the shrubs like a circus acrobat. Its quarry was still mainly hoverflies, which were being attracted by the ivy blossom. It would dart, hang upside down and catch one with amazing agility. I did hear it call. It gave a little murmur, a soft 'chack' of delight every time it pinioned another hoverfly. Its call was far less harsh than that of the Dusky Warbler.

Having enjoyed further views of the Olivaceous Warbler at leisure, I walked back in the direction of Longstones again. At the head of Holy Vale five birders were looking over a gate into a field. Beyond, a couple of cows were grazing peacefully, but there seemed to be no evidence of anything else exciting to attract them. I came to the conclusion they were just scanning, so wandered on towards Longstones. When I arrived there I heard that a Grey-headed Wagtail had just been seen in the field at the top of Holy Vale. That must have been the attraction in the field with the cows, I thought to myself and decided to go back.

"Is it still there?" I enquired as I arrived.

"Yes", a birder replied, making room for me at the gate. "It's hopping about just in front of that cow's left front leg. You can't actually see it at the moment, though." I found the relevant cow's leg. There were plenty of ordinary Yellow Wagtails picking up disturbed insects from around the cow's feet, but nothing more exciting. After five minutes or so, one of the other birders announced, "There it is...about four feet in front of the leading cow's front legs." I scanned with my binoculars and quickly found it. It was a startling, well-marked little bird, but of course it's only a race of a Yellow Wagtail and therefore untickable. Another attractive bird, which appeared on Scilly in 1984, was a Siberian Stonechat. It only occurs in Britain occasionally, but as it was then just a race of Common Stonechat very few people took the trouble to go and see it. The Grey-headed Wagtail was black immediately around the eye, then the black graded into grey towards the forehead and around the nape of the neck. I enjoyed it for some time before I left.

The light was beginning to fade, and my birding time on Scilly fading with it. I thought I might as well stroll back to town via Telegraph Hill just in case that wretched Richard's Pipit had decided to put in an appearance. There was neither sign of it, nor of birders searching for it. That was that then. It had been a pleasant day, but there had been nothing new except for the Grey-headed Wagtail. In spite of the fact that this was my first visit to Scilly, I would be leaving the islands tomorrow very much a today's man.

When I arrived back in town I made my way up to Greystones and organised my things. I paid off various bills, did various boring things like my share of the washing up and hoarding dirty socks. Once everything was more or less ready, I went down to the Mermaid and bid the Scillies farewell with an excellent Beef Stroganoff. Scilly birding may have finished for me, but Clive and I were off early in the morning as we had planned a full day birding in mainland Cornwall which could be very productive. I was also still very keen to do some more sea watching. Two of the best sea watching headlands in Britain are St. Ives and Porthgwarra in Western Cornwall, and I was keen to give them a try. Clive was not so keen. Sea watching is best earlier in the autumn and by the end of October; it was unlikely that there would be anything very interesting flying past. Others told us that we should go and look at the Golden Plover flock at St Just. Apparently the Lesser Golden Plover, which Chris and Tessa had tried for on their way down, was still there. Otherwise there was a Little Egret in Plymouth and vague rumours of an American Redstart.

About halfway through the evening, a young lad came into the Mermaid in a desperate state. His face was positively ashen.

"Have you heard the dreadful news?" he spluttered.

"No, what's that?" we asked through beer fumes and a friendly haze of cigarette smoke.

"Something really terrible has happened", he continued.

"Here, calm down, have a seat...a beer?" we suggested soothingly. "It can't be as bad as all that, surely?"

"It is", he assured us, his complexion turning yet a few shades paler. "A Black-throated Blue Warbler's been found in the gutter outside the 'Cressa. It's the first for Britain, and it got itself squashed by a car before anyone's even had a chance to tick it. What a terrible waste", he wailed. "To make matters worse, if that were possible it's a male. A male in full adult plumage. It would have been an utterly stonking bird, but now it's gone. Why couldn't it have waited until I'd ticked it before flying beneath that bloody car."

Oh well, I thought to myself, that's a shame. However, I thought the corpse might be worth seeing, so I asked the lad where it was.

"It's in The Bishop and Wolf", he groaned. The Bishop and Wolf is another birders' pub, just a hundred yards down the High Street from the Mermaid. As I made my way along the High Street I noticed it was now drizzling. When I got to the pub the lads told me that it was now lying in state in the Porthcressa.

In the Porthcressa, down at the birders' bar in the basement, I found it – a very two-dimensional mummified bird – lying on a piece of A4 paper in the middle of a table. I had expected to see something damp and fresh, with a few entrails oozing from it at the very least. It was raining outside, but this corpse was as dry as dust. I became suspicious to say the least.

At the time I was a professional museum curator and head of a county museum service biology department.

"I hope someone's thought to collect the parasites", I remarked, feeling suddenly authoritative. "If it's still got some it could be authenticated as a genuine American vagrant and not a cage bird which has escaped." All my training as someone who deals with important natural history specimens came to the fore. "If it is genuinely British, it's a very important specimen and ought to go to the Natural History Museum." Just then, a very well-known member of the Rarities Committee sidled across and told us that it was indeed a genuine transatlantic vagrant. He admitted that it had made the crossing...in his suitcase!

"Trouble is, it's making quite a stir", he went on. "I believe they've even got hold of the story in Nancy's." When I arrived back at the Mermaid and told the young lad the truth of the story, his face positively glowed with relief.

16. *The return journey*

Clive and I had ordered a taxi to take us up to the airport for the nine fifteen helicopter. We heaved our cases out of the bungalow and waited for the taxi. We scanned the dew covered playing fields in case a Pink Stink or Richard's had decided to arrive over night. There were plenty of Meadow Pipits, but little else.

All too soon the taxi arrived. We put our cases on board and were whisked up to the airport. It was galling that we were the first members of our group to be leaving, but Clive and I both had reasons to be home early. The strong wind of the last couple of days had abated. That wind must have brought something to Scilly...and it had! I was to hear of it two days later and be thoroughly gripped off.

When we got to the airport we scanned the fields before going into the departure lounge. The St. Mary's departure lounge is fractionally more luxurious than the one in Penzance, though the difference was marginal. Other passengers waited in stony-faced silence for the helicopter to arrive from Penzance. None were birders: we were the only ones going the wrong way it seemed. The helicopter arrived, we boarded and flew back to Penzance. Once again, I was glad we were not sailing with the *Scillonian*. The sea looked uninvitingly grey and threatening beneath us.

When we arrived in Penzance we collected our cases and went to find Clive's car. To our surprise and delight it started without difficulty. The first thing to do was to go to St. Just and locate the Golden Plover flock. Driving out of Penzance, we noticed an autumnal freshness in the air, which had been absent in Scilly. How depressing! The grass on St. Just airfield was covered in a variety of wax cap fungi, which are always a sign of approaching winter.

There was no sign of any Golden Plovers, however. We had just started to return to the car when another car passed us plastered in birders' stickers. It slowed down and stopped. The driver must have noticed Clive's telescope in the back of his car and recognised fellow birders. We rushed up to the car, and they told us where to find the Golden Plover flock. We drove off there and found a large undulating pasture on a hillside.

"Can you feel a tick coming on?" I asked Clive as we scanned the flock of around eighty Golden Plover. Although my new binoculars were quite good, I could find nothing different about any of the birds in the flock. Clive began to scan each bird in the flock methodically with his telescope. He had scanned about half of the flock when they all took off. They flew around the field in formation and, after about five minutes or so, flew in low and landed in more or less the same area. We started scanning again, and this time I found a bird which I thought looked a little different. Clive had just found the bird in his telescope when they all flew off again.

"What do you think, Clive?" I asked.

"No", he replied quite definitely. "That's not a Lesser. It's not nearly grey enough. What we're looking for is a much greyer bird with more contrast between the wings and the belly. In fact, it looks more like a Grey Plover." This time they flew off and didn't return. Apparently the flock moved between St. Just and the coastal village of Sennen, so we decided to drive there and see if we could locate the rest of the flock. The whole flock was supposed to consist of more than three hundred birds. We didn't have to drive far before we arrived in Sennen Cove but were unable to relocate the smaller flock, let alone the rest of them. The sea looked rough, and the wind was blowing parallel to the cove. Ideal sea watching conditions, I thought to myself. A quick glance took in about a dozen Gannets. Perhaps I was going to have a sea watch after all. Outside the car the wind was terrific. A black cloud out to sea promised a squally shower any minute. The white of the Gannets contrasted starkly with the huge black waves, looking as though they were made of ivory. Many of the Gannets were coming in very close to the shore.

"Clive", I asked. "Is there a technique for sea watching?"

"Yeah, what I do is to scan the sea in the direction the birds are flying just a little faster than they are going past. I tell you what. You scan the closer sea with your bins, and I'll try further out with the 'scope."

Amongst the Gannets there were Kittiwakes, but none of them proved to be Sabine's Gulls. Flocks of auks flew past like bullets. Most were unidentifiable, but those that were proved to be Common Guillemot. Little groups of Turnstone and Purple Sandpiper fluttered low, skimming fast over the waves. The sea was alive with birds. I hadn't been scanning long when I picked up a large dark brown bird with distinctive carpel patches.

"Great Skua I think, Clive", I announced and gave him directions. That was the best view I had ever had of a Bonxie, as they are often called, especially in Scotland. It was also the best bird we saw. Clive picked out two other skuas, most probably Arctic, but they were too far out to sea to be sure. After a couple of hours we called it a day and went into a nearby pub for lunch.

"Let's go and give that Lesser another go", I suggested to Clive when we had finished our lunch. "It's worth a try, and there's nothing else to do."

"Okay", he replied and we drove back to the field. As we

arrived, a very much larger flock of Golden Plover flew up. They wheeled around several times, looking like a shoal of frightened fish in a tropical sea. First they would be brown dots, then, as they moved, they flashed silver in unison against the threatening grey cloud behind. After a few moments, they came in to land very low across the field in front of us. Unfortunately, they had mostly landed in dead ground, screened from us by a slight rise in the field. We could just make out a few brown blobs, which were the heads of the closest birds.

"Damn!" I cursed loudly. "Come on Clive. We're not on Scilly now. Let's creep along the hedge until we can get a better position and a decent view. If someone does come along, we can always plead the ignorance of a visitor to the area and apologise." This was very naughty and unethical, but I was anxious to see that bird.

We moved carefully along the hedge, and, sure enough, the whole flock came into view. Clearly this was the whole flock; there were many more birds now than there had been earlier that morning. I started to scan the flock, but with binoculars all I could see was a conglomeration of brown blobs. The wind was fierce, and tears rolled down my cheeks making scanning very tricky. Clive scanned with his telescope.

After about ten minutes, I asked Clive how he was getting on.

"About three quarters of the way through", he replied. "No sign yet, I'm afraid."

"Let's have a quick look", I asked. I now appreciated the enormity of Clive's task. Admittedly, the birds were larger through the telescope, but my eyes were watering even more profusely because of the concentration and the wind. Matters were made worse because the strong wind caused the tripod to vibrate. All I could see were vibrating birds jiggering up and down.

"Here Clive, I can't manage this, you'd better carry on", I suggested. It must have been another three or four minutes before Clive whispered quietly.

"I think I've got it...yes!" he announced confidently. "That's the Lesser." At that very moment, I spotted a Buzzard flying fast towards the flock and I knew precisely what was going to happen. I scarcely had time to whisper desperately, "Quick Clive, let's have a look", before the whole flock lifted.

"It's definitely a Lesser", Clive enthused, reaffirming his diagnosis. "I saw its black armpits as it took off."

"Great!" I replied sarcastically. "It's alright for some." Was this to be yet another grip off? This time it would be me on the receiving end. The whole flock wheeled round once and then flew out over the sea gradually getting higher and higher, and always moving further and further away from us. Somewhere up there was a Lesser Golden Plover, but there was absolutely no knowing which of the myriad black dots it was. Just before the flock disappeared into the distant mists, it split into two. Moments later, another smaller flock came to join one of the halves, then this flock split again into two further, more or less, equal halves.

"If they come back, and the wrong half returns", I muttered bitterly, "It'll be enough to make me give up birding." I spent a most unhappy five minutes before one of the halves of the flock returned. It wheeled round tantalisingly. From time to time it looked very much as though it would fly off again. Five minutes later they came in to land in the field. This time they landed closer and well below the horizon.

"Come on, Clive", I cajoled. "Let's go right round to the other side of the field. From there the light won't be shining into our eyes, and it might even be more sheltered; we should be able to get much closer." We made our way to the other side of the field in a wide arc. We started to scan again. I had been right. The birds were much easier to see from this new vantage point. I hadn't been at it long when I picked out a distinctly neater, greyer bird.

"Clive", I whispered tentatively, "I think I've got it." I gave him directions, and he found my bird in his telescope.

"Yes, that's it."

"Thank goodness for that!" I let out a huge sigh of relief. It had been a difficult bird, and, in the end, I had found it for myself. In many ways, it was one of the most enjoyable ticks of the trip.

"Well, that's that, I suppose", I sighed with resignation, and it was pretty well. We drove towards Plymouth and the more major roads taking us east towards Dorset and Christchurch. We had been away from civilization and the modern world for a fortnight, and the effect of our return was a considerable culture shock. Briefly we tried for the Little Egret at Wembury near Plymouth, but without success. As we got nearer Christchurch, I was grateful as it dawned on me that Clive's driving had improved considerably. By the time we arrived home, I was almost relaxed.

Postscript

Three days later I rang Chris and Tessa who had also arrived back in Christchurch by then.

"Come on, Chris", I urged him. "Give us the worst. Grip me off and tell me what you had after we left."

"Are you really sure you want to hear?" he replied smoothly. I wasn't sure at all and felt an uncomfortable feeling rising in the pit of my stomach.

"Okay, come on", I answered. "Let's get it over with."

"Well, on the last day most of the others went off to Tresco to see a Red-throated Pipit. Tessa and I didn't need it, so we thought we might as well amble off up to Salakee Farm. You know, just below the airport."

"Yes, I know, go on." I interrupted.

"We arrived there just as an Eyebrowed Thrush was found. Stonking bird…crippling views…"

"Rats!"

Gripped off again. Still, there was always another year, but that's another story.

The future. A Bobolink arrives at St. Mary's Airport in 1985.

Acknowledgements

I should very much like to thank the Tessa of this book, who kindly made a first typescript for me from my manuscript.

I should also like to thank Richard Millington and Group-Captain Peter Symonds who both read and commented on earlier drafts of this book.

I also thank Hugh and Nicola Loxdale from Brambleby Books for their careful editing of the text.

The names of the real people described in the book have been changed, except for those of well-known and established figures in the world of birds.

References Cited in Text

Birding World. Monthly magazine published by the Bird Information Service 1987-present

Grant, P. J. (1982), *Gulls: A Guide to Identification*. Poyser

Millington, R. (1981), *A Twitcher's Diary: the Birdwatching Year of Richard Millington*. Blandford, London.

Oddie, W. E. (1982), *Bill Oddie's Little Black Bird Book*. Mandarin
(New version published 2011)

Scott, S. L. (Ed) (1983), *National Geographic Field Guide to the Birds of North America*. National Geographic Society, Washington D. C. (Current version published 2011: Sixth Edition)

Further Reading

Parslow, R. (2007), *The Isles of Scilly*. HarperCollins, London. The New Naturalist Library 103.

Other birding books by Brambleby Books

Arrivals and Rivals – A duel for the winning bird
Adrian Riley
ISBN 9780954334796

UK500: Birding in the fast lane
James Hanlon
ISBN 9780954334789

Winging it – Birding for Low-flyers
Andrew Fallan
ISBN 9780955392856

The Ruffled Edge – Notes from a Nature Warden
Pete Howard
ISBN 9781908241061

Birduder 344 – A life list ordinary
Rob Sawyer
ISBN 9781908241092

A-Z of Birds – A birder's tale from around the world
Bo Beolens
ISBN 9781908241238

Sheer Cliffs and Shearwaters – A Skomer Island Journal
Richard Kipling
ISBN 9781908241214

Walking with Birds
Colin Whittle
ISBN 9781908241351

www.bramblebybooks.co.uk